The

Mr.& Mrs.

HAPPY HANDBOOK

The
Mr.& Mrs.
HAPPY HANDBOOK

Everything I Know About
Love and Marriage

STEVE DOOCY
(with corrections by Mrs. Doocy)

■ HarperLargePrint
An Imprint of HarperCollins*Publishers*
www.harpercollins.com

HarperLargePrint
An Imprint of HarperCollins Publishers
10 East 53rd Street
New York, NY 10022.

ISBN-10: 0-06-124259-4
ISBN-13: 978-0-06-124259-5

Printed in the U.S.A.

10 9 8 7 6 5 4 3 2 1

This Large Print Book carries
the Seal of Approval of N.A.V.H.

To Kathy, Peter, Mary, and Sally,
thanks for making me Mr. Happy

Contents

INTRODUCTION   1

chapter one: In the Beginning...   7

For His Eyes Only: Ladies, Please
    Skip This Passage   9

My Date with Destiny: October 27, 1985   10

chapter two: The Wedding and
    the Honeymoon   19

Our Wedding Day: Countdown to Cake   20

George of the Wedding Jungle: W's Dos
    and Don'ts   25

What's a Honeymoon? A History Lesson   28

Adam and Steve: My Accidental
    Honeymoon   30

Lovers and Lepers: My Honeymoon
    with Meg Ryan   35

Honeymoon Horror Story: The Man
    from Glad   42

Porn to Be Wild: Should You Camcorder
    Everything?   42

A for Effort: Grading the Honeymoon   45

chapter three: Marriage   49

You're Mr. & Mrs. Happy: Now What?   49

What We Really Want: The Lowdown
    on Love   52

I Can See Clearly Now: The End of the
    Honeymoon Effect   52

From "I Do" to "Uh-oh": Retraining
    the New Hire   53

Wedding Caher: I Married a Cheapskate   59

Love Me (Legal) Tender: Marrieds
    and Money   62

Tastes Like Chicken: The Fear Factor   67

The Edit Sweet: Honesty   70

Married to the Mom: In-laws   74

I Dropped When I Shopped: Gift Fatigue   79

Saturday-Night Fights: How to Argue
    Without Gunplay   83

Oh No, It's Geraldo! When There's an
    Age Difference   87

Rules of Engagement: Married in
the Military 93

Gimme Shelter: Your First Home 98

A Moving Experience: Relocating
Your Family 101

The Aliens Next Door: Your Neighbors 109

Mr. Handy: Home Remodeling 114

King of Pain: Should I Go to the Hospital? 120

When I'm Dead, She's Rich:
Wife Insurance 124

Pet of the Year: Animal House 127

Volun-teers of a Clown: Public Service 133

Good Sports: Playing Together 139

Our Marriage Is Perfect, Let's Date!
An Experiment 143

chapter four: Kids 149

Growing Your Family Tree: What Are
You In For? 149

Pee on the Stick: Pregnancy 152

Dial M for Mother: Delivery Day 158

Sorry, Tallulah's Taken: Naming the Baby 165

Breast Intentions: Feeding in Public   170

Fear Factor: Baby Monitoring   174

Nannygate: Finding a Babysitter   180

Say What? Kids Say the Darnedest Things   186

Parent Trap: A Parent's Pop Quiz   190

Making the Grade: Time for School   196

My Boy in the Bubble: Are You
Too Protective?   203

Where Did We Go Wrong?
Worst-Case Scenarios   208

Crime and Punishment: Discipline   210

The Birds, the Bees, the Carrot:
Talking About Sex   216

Dine and Dash: Feeding Time   221

Frequent-Crier Miles: Traveling with Kids   228

Almost Rubbed Out by Rudolph:
Freak Accidents   232

My Father the Spy, My Mother the
Murderer: What Parents Do
for Their Kids   239

Be Prepared: Girl and Boy Scouts   244

The Coach Bag: Going Out for the Team   256

The Graduate: Kids and College   265

chapter five: Mature Topics   275

Where Do I Plug This In? Appliances   275

I Love You, You're Perfect, Now Wear
    This Thong: Do Not Attempt
    This at Home   276

The Love Machine, by Kenmore:
    Mom and Dad Take a Time-out   278

Porn Losers: When You See Things
    You Should Not   280

Me Tarzan, You Neighbor: Swingers   283

chapter six: Troubleshooting   285

Kill Him with Kindness: Desperate
    Housewives   285

The Doctor Is In, the Parking Lot:
    Affairs   289

When It Hits the Fan: Kathie Lee
    and Frank Gifford   293

Mother of All Arguments: The Prenup   296

chapter seven: Happily Ever After   303

Cracking the Code: The Secret to a
    Long, Happy Marriage   303

"Yes, Dear, Pour Me a Beer": The
   Longest Marriage on Earth   305

Honeymooner Hall of Fame: Real-Life
   Success Stories   307

Peggy Sue Got Married: Marrying Your
   High School Sweetheart   311

The 4-H Club: Recipe for a Happy
   Marriage   315

Where's the Tabasco? How to Keep
   Marriage Exciting   319

The Not-So-Newlywed Game: Five
   Questions for Your Spouse   321

Niagara Falls Plus Fifty: Good News:
   Love Lasts   322

I'M ALMOST OUT OF TONER:
   FINAL THOUGHTS   327

AUTHOR THANK-YOUS AND
   SHOUT-OUTS   333

Introduction

I was eight when a grown man in khaki shorts and black knee socks presented me with a book that would change my life: **The Boy Scout Handbook.** The secrets of the world, in one squat two-pound reference book. Over the next few years I'd use it to learn how to build a campfire without matches, the correct way to wear the neckerchief, and a skill I still use every day, correct knot tying. If you spot me leaving Home Depot with lumber on my roof this weekend, you can bet it's secured to my car with a clove hitch.

When I was twelvish, the handbook was losing its edge. I'd learned only half of the semaphore alphabet, which made sending dirty messages practically impossible. And a young man with bubbling hormones can only be captivated by **Boy's Life** magazine for so long. That's when I realized that if **The Boy Scout Handbook** was to show me how to "be prepared" for the life ahead, where was the chapter on **Girl** Scouts? There wasn't one. And what about the Girl Scouts organization—were they preparing young women to meet young men? No, they were training future women how to be contestants on **The Apprentice** by thinking of 101 ways to sell Thin Mints.

When we proudly took our first child home from the hospital, I remember my wife turning to me in the car with a worried look I'd never seen before, saying, "We need an **owner's manual** for this kid." It would have been useful in figuring out how to change his oil.

In the many years since I retired my Boy Scout Totin' Chip, I've longed for a book of common-sense stories that would preview and advise me on the quasi-mysterious parts of life. Think of this book as an operator's manual for marriage, children, and family. (The pet stuff is an added bonus.)

We all crave help; however, there is no centralized authority on this stuff. We'd like to think that **somebody** knows all. That person probably has a stentorian voice and a silvery head of hair and wears an ascot. Unfortunately, Phil Donahue won't return your phone calls.

So realistically, from whom do people get advice? Sadly, many turn to their gabby neighbor whose greatest married achievement is teaching his wife to do that maraschino-cherry trick…or a radio show host who's been married four times. That seems to be what the cultural tennis-ball machine is firing at us these days.

This is not an advice book per se (Latin for per se) because what worked for me and the many people I've interviewed for this book may not work for you. It's more of a DON'T TRY THIS AT HOME book. We've already made almost every conceivable mistake and can save you the wear and tear of being an idiot yourself.

I bring to the book nook the practical advice of a man married twenty **consecutive** years, to the same wonderful woman who two decades ago made a clean break with reality and married me. (Editor's Note: Insert Steve's current wife's name here.)

Kathy. Saint Kathy.

"You look like a happy person" is what George W. Bush said to my wife when the Secret Service accidentally allowed us into the White House. Secretary of Defense Donald Rumsfeld, who in spite of having several years on me could still snap my neck like a toothpick, took one look at me and then a long look at my wife and pronounced, "It looks like you married up, son." Then he asked my wife if she was interested in enlisting in the army, and she said, "Only if they have Pilates."

There are also plenty of stories about those short people who share your house and want stuff—kids. Followed by chapters on mature topics and troubleshooting for tricky times when the warning light on your dashboard o' love is flashing. Finally, a few wise words on the getting to the "happily ever after" part. This thorough manual covers everything from honeymoon to last rites.

Here are some of the things you'll learn about if you're lucky and/or paying attention:

- Why the only time you can be 100 percent sure your spouse is telling the truth involves a strong narcotic and a long hose
- My accidental honeymoon with a man, and my eventual real honeymoon with my wife, Meg Ryan
- A wealthy husband who buried his own mother in a wholesale casket
- Our $327,090 dog
- How a neighbor's kid started a cockfight in our living room
- What happened when my wife and I joined an online dating service to prove that we were meant for each other. Despite the fact that our one-month experiment ended last year, she's still getting e-mailed photos of single men whose photos appear to have been taken at a skinhead convention. Luckily she still prefers bonehead to skinhead.

These stories are true. They involved either me or one of my soon-to-be-ex-friends. Because I work on a daily live TV show, some of my friends are really famous people from the worlds of entertainment, politics, and business. A series of these celebrities confessed sidesplitting marriage stories, each a potential **National Enquirer** headline. When I asked for permission to print them in this book, in one way or another, most made it clear: "You can't use my name!" because, in the words of one luminary, "My fans would think I'm a nincompoop!" Many boldfaced names were reluctant to spill their glamorous guts because the last thing they need is to be heckled on the next red carpet.

"Hey, (Famous Name)! Your wife says you hate to pull over on long road trips and you pee into a Gatorade bottle! Gag! Now get to the back of the gift-bag line!"

To protect their lucrative show-business careers, I am not using most of their names. So I will neither confirm nor deny whether the story about the can of Pam cooking spray and the rubber wedding dress is about Brian Kilmeade.

I hope you enjoy **The Mr. & Mrs. Happy Handbook**. If you're the one person who doesn't, I bet your spouse does, and that's the problem with you two! Look, nobody has the perfect marriage, because perfect is impossible. The best you can hope for is a happy marriage. This book is a collection of my eyewitness reportage from twenty-five years as a professional journalist on what makes marriages happy.

You happily picked your spouse for a terrific reason—in your heart you felt like the two of you were a perfect fit. Just like my grandma always told me, "Every pot will find its lid." She also said, "Stop poking that cat with a stick!" but the pot thing seemed like a better way to kick off a non-pet book.

chapter one

In the Beginning…

Throughout history men have had problems dealing with women.

"Do I look fat in this fig leaf?" Eve asked Adam.

Adam, a born kidder, promptly puffed up his cheeks and belted out a deep-throated "Moooooooo!" Eve was puzzled. God hadn't invented cows yet—he was still working out the bugs on the passenger pigeon. She instinctively found his cringeworthy performance offensive. Adam was officially in the doghouse, which was tricky, because there were no dogs. God was only in the B's, working on birds.

The world hasn't changed that much in the thousands of years since fig leaves and Adams and Eves, although now there are also plenty of Adams and Steves, just not in this book. Today's guys believe they understand girls and vice versa, but really men know as much about women as golden retrievers know about Roth IRAs.

There are plenty of differences between the sexes. We are clearly wired differently. It's first noticeable when we're boys and girls. For instance, when my wife presented my daughters with their first bras, they were horrified. One daughter refused to wear it, and kept hiding it under her bed. Finally, when asked why she wouldn't wear it, the ten-year-old looked her straight in the eye and in the voice of Peter Pan said, "Think happy thoughts, Mommy."

Meanwhile, when my immodest son made the high school baseball team, he came down to the dinner table to model his cup.

As we mature, the differences multiply. Just look at how our brains work. Men generally have direct, basic questions:

- "Will this make me gassy?"
- "Are you sure this won't show up as porn on the hotel bill?"

Women's questions are more complicated and fraught with emotional subterfuge. Like this one that is apparently programmed in all women at the factory to test the depth of a man's love and honesty.

- "Do I look fat in these pants?"

This has nothing to do with pants, and guys don't know where to start. They'll pause half a moment to think, but during his momentary hesitation, the woman's paranoid gland secretes a trace hormone into her bloodstream that immediately translates, "He thinks I'm fat!"

That leads to sheets of tears, prolonged awkward apologies, and the dreaded but inevitable "Twice yearly."

It's time for men and women to realize that despite his occasional affinity for lavender soap, he is still all man. She should know she is living with a mammal that is just one cultural chromosome away from being a coyote. He doesn't get the charm of children's beauty pageants, tiny dogs in designer footwear, or a purse that costs more than the average daily bank balance.

Rather than truly understand each other, they inevitably smile with gritted teeth and pretend they didn't hear the latest dumb thing their spouse just blurted out. Both sexes need to stop making the same mistakes and move on.

"Insanity," the old expression goes, "is doing the same thing and expecting different results."

FOR HIS EYES ONLY

Ladies, Please Skip This Passage

When your spouse asks, "Do I look fat in these pants/dress/fig leaf?" there is but one simple answer that will lead to a long and happy marriage: **"No habla ingles"** (translation: "I don't speak English").

By the time she translates and realizes that she's now mad at you for not answering her question, you're off the hook. She's forgotten about her tight pants.

Why Do People Get Married?

52%: "We're in love"
23%: To get pushy parents off their backs
15%: So they won't go to hell for having sex
8%: Various (financial, security, lonely, hooked on multilayered cake)
2%: Want to find out their blood type

MY DATE WITH DESTINY

October 27, 1985

I was sitting with my sister Lisa at the bar of Stetson's, a Tex-Mex joint in Washington, D.C. We were watching our team, the Kansas City Royals, clinch the seventh game of the World Series. As the MVP was interviewed by a cute blond dugout reporter, I mentioned to my sister that the sports girl on TV had just started working in my building.

"She's cute," Lisa said. "Why don't you ask her out?"

"That girl? She's too fabulous for me."

Actually, she was too fabulous for everybody. She was a Ford model and the first woman on ESPN to have her own magazine show. She'd never met a double black diamond she couldn't master and she'd dated or was pals with six of the ten men listed that year in **People** magazine's first "Sexiest Man Alive" poll. On top of that, she was painfully beautiful.

"Yeah, you're right," my sister said. "You're low tide in the gene pool compared to her."

Now you know why I moved away from home.

A week later I saw Miss Too Fabulous for Me in the NBC commissary. She had on her tray an oozing cheeseburger, a supersized order of French fries, a salad, a cookie, and a Diet Coke. For a size 6, she ate like a Teamster.

It's hard to try to make small talk with a cute girl when she's in line sandwiched between Roger Mudd and Connie Chung, so I didn't. I just stood quietly in line as if I were idling in the drive-up lane at Wendy's.

She disappeared out the door.

As I was at the fork, spoon, knife station, she popped back in and quickly grabbed two packets of salt, which at that time was still free at NBC (prebudget cuts).

Suddenly I was walking down the hall with her toward our desks, and I knew I really should say something. A good pickup line would have been "I only have three months to live, kiss me!" Instead I asked, "What's that stuff on your fries? Plasma?"

Pitiful, but it engaged her. She cracked an icy smile and responded, "We call it ketchup."

As a doctor's office reader of **Cosmo,** I knew girls love compliments, so I quickly followed up with "You did a great job at the World Series."

"Thanks."

"I'm from Kansas. I like the Royals."

"That's nice." Yes, the Lame-O-Meter indicator was peaking, until she finally joined the conversation.

"My boss says you're a womanizer," she said, in that same tone Marcia Clark used to grill Kato Kaelin.

"Really?" I said, stunned.

"You've dated every woman at NBC, and you've been seen lurking over at CBS."

"That's not true!" (It was ABC.)

She turned a corner and vanished.

Doomed, right? Not so fast. After a month of her giving me weird mercy glances in the hall, we found ourselves, as junior members of the staff, working that lonely week between Christmas and New Year's. Noonish on December 31, I saw her with her Dumpster of death leaving the cafeteria.

"Happy New Year's," she said.

For a change **she** had initiated the conversation, and then she stopped. This was my chance. "Right back at ya," I said. "So what's your plan for tonight?"

She said she was working the late news shift and wouldn't be off until eleven-thirty. "You want to get together?" she inquired.

Eleven-thirty that night? Six hours after my workday was done? "Sure," I said calmly, while my insides did that victory dance one does after Ed McMahon presents somebody with a big cardboard check.

"Great," she said, gave me her address, and **poof!** She was gone again.

As I was heading out the door, my boss asked me if I could do a live report from downtown Washington at 11 P.M. I paused. Actually, that would work out great. I'd get off the same time as the girl, and I'd be tanked up on coffee and ready for fun.

At 11:05, moments after my live report, I was ready to zip back to the studio to pick up my date, but a producer at the network called to see if I could stick around and do a live report at midnight during **The Tonight Show (starring) Johnny Carson**.

"Are you kidding? Of course I'll stick around. Just one thing..." This was a pre–cell phone era, and I asked the producer if he'd call my date and tell her I'd be late.

"Sure, no problem," he said, and he hung up and simultaneously forgot to place the call.

It was almost midnight, and my date had dashed home, showered, changed, and was ready. All she needed was me. She called my office, my house, a friend—nobody knew where I was. As she waited she turned on the television. Normally she watched Dick Clark, but now that she worked for "the other network," she flipped to the peacock.

And there in living color was the guy from the cafeteria. She'd been stood up before, but never on network television. That was a first.

As the clock ticked toward midnight, I was surrounded by about a hundred thousand people, and thankfully two were sober. About a dozen of the really drunk ones thought it would be hilarious if they started to rock the TV truck back and forth. That normally would be funny, but I was on top of it, and I looked like I was doing a live report from the deck of an ocean liner in fifty-foot swells. The only difference, when you're on a cruise ship they don't throw beer bottles at you. But they were coming at me fast and furious. One hit the telescoping pole that sends the signal back to the station, and it shattered next to me, giving me a dandy brown-glass shampoo.

A hundred feet away, the hardest-working man in show business, James Brown, was counting down, "Three-two-one, Happy New Year! I feel good. I knew that I would now."

I, on the other hand, did not feel good. I felt terrible. Because of the police lines and overflow crowd, I couldn't get back in time for my date. With one boozy live shot I'd moved from the penthouse to the outhouse.

The next day I called her to apologize. She told me she'd seen me and completely understood.

"Did that beer bottle hit you in the head?" she asked. I was touched by her concern. I was even more surprised that when I asked her for a raincheck the next day, she said yes. Our flatlined friendship had just been revived with one jolt of the paddles.

We planned to get together with a friend of mine and his wife; they were very colorful characters, and I thought it would be fun. My date wore a new blue suede suit. She was stunning. Upon review I'm positive that her beauty overwhelmed my motor skills, because during the course of the dinner I spilled a glass of red wine on her lap, and over dessert, I soaked her with a cup of coffee.

She was furious. This date had crashed on takeoff and the NTSB was now looking for the black boxes. At the end of the night, I asked her if I could walk her to her door.

"No, that's really not necessary."

Sensing my date with the cutest girl I'd ever met could end with a knife wound, I stopped at her stoop and threw myself on the mercy of the court. I apologized for everything. Standing her up, ruining her clothes, inviting my friends, who sent the wine back **twice** and then got into an argument that ended with the wife asking a waiter for a ride home. I took complete responsibility for everything bad that happened that day, including the Dow Jones Industrial Average dropping thirty-seven points. (Greenspan taught me that one.)

I waited for her reaction. "Please say something," I begged silently. "Anything." She just stood there giving me an X-ray look as if trying to see if there was a brain in my head, because so far she'd not seen anything to conclude that there was. Finally she broke radio silence. "Do you want to come in for a drink?"

This wasn't the dream sequence; it really happened. I was so relieved. I was also thirsty, and almost positive she had dry clothes I hadn't ruined yet, so I accepted her offer.

Over the bottle of champagne she'd bought for New Year's, we laughed about the dinner catastrophe. When that was exhausted, we moved into the expected aimless small talk, until we started discussing our jobs and then our families. We talked all night. I learned her life story. She listened to mine. We connected in a way I'd never expected. After about five hours of talking, it was official: I liked her a lot. She was exactly the girl I'd dreamed I'd marry and live with in a bungalow on a quiet street with our three children and our Lassie. (Petwise it was hard to beat a dog with a show in the top ten.)

After ten hours of talking she had to shoo me out of her apartment. "I've got to go to work. You should go."

As I walked to the door, I ad-libbed a good-bye that shocked even me. "I know this is gonna scare you," I said, "but someday, we'll be married."

That's when she gave me the look David Kaczynski probably gave his brother Ted when he realized he was the Unabomber. "That's nice. You should really leave now."

Forty-one days later I proposed at table 52 at the Washington Palm.

Six months and twenty-eight days later we were married.

That was twenty years ago.

chapter two

The Wedding and the Honeymoon

I saw a quote from H. Jackson Brown Jr. on a poster or a refrigerator magnet that said, "Marry the right person. This one decision will determine 90 percent of your happiness or misery."

We ask ourselves, "Is this the right person?"

When I asked it, I had to make a choice: should I go with the blonde or the red? Because I was thinking about proposing marriage just six weeks after our first date, a lot of my previous life plans were suddenly in limbo. I'd been a bachelor for years, and I had wanted to treat myself to an expensive red sports car.

I had a choice: buy a big ring, get married, and go into debt, or buy a red car, get a lot of speeding tickets, and go into debt. I was going to be broke one way or the other—it was a matter of whether I'd get there via the hot rod or the rock.

"Wow, I guess you're not getting the Porsche" is what my friend M.J. said when she saw the ice on my fiancée's finger.

Of course love always prevails. I got the rock, proposed to the blonde, and we drove off to a new life in my 1979 Ford Pinto (please don't tailgate). It was the best decision I ever made. Luckily it turns out she's not a gas guzzler.

I'm still waiting for the red car, which I intend to get at the commencement of my midlife crisis, which will start the moment my wife gives me permission. I envision her giving me the "It's okay with me" wave of her left hand, which is where my red convertible has been parked for the past twenty years.

OUR WEDDING DAY

Countdown to Cake

Justice of the Peace: $75
Rent-a-harpist: $125
Case of Chandon sparkling wine: $84
Rose Garden Pavilion, Loose Park, Kansas
    City, Missouri: Free
Total cost of our wedding: $284
Getting married in a public park ninety
    seconds before a thunderstorm rolls in:
    Priceless

There are some things money can't buy; a happy wedding is one of them.

We really did spend less than three hundred bucks to get hitched. Luckily we had help—my new brothers-in-law picked up the reception tab, which was a lot because I come from a family of drinkers. My father paid the bill at Gates Barbecue for our rehearsal dinner where the most expensive item was six dollars. And my mother insisted on bringing the cake. The three-tiered lemon cake filled with vanilla buttercream was baked in my hometown of Abilene, Kansas. My mom and dad transported it 180 miles to Kansas City's Loose Park on the spare tire in the trunk of the family K-car. The three-hour drive was during an incredible heat spell in the Midwest, and it never dawned on them that the trunk was not air-conditioned. When Dad went around back to open the trunk he knew something was wrong when he noticed frosting dripping out by the muffler. I thought it was funny that my mom promised cake, but wound up bringing wedding soup. She felt terrible until we tapped into the case of wine that switched off the voice of Betty Crocker scolding her in her head.

A helpful waiter at the reception offered some consolation. "How about if everybody gets a straw?" he guffawed. My mother gave him a subzero stare that sent him into the kitchen. He later returned to the table with a single-layer cake. It looked fine, despite the steel belted radial aftertaste.

Our wedding with just fifteen guests was splendid in its simplicity. So different from one of my friends who had a wedding with 205 guests and an unlimited budget. But bigger isn't always better. The bride's father recommended a famous photographer who'd worked at **National Geographic.** She hired him thinking of that magazine's famous nature shots and compelling images of humanity, but as it turned out this photographer's specialty was not people, it was capturing erupting volcanoes.

The celebrity shutterbug had never done a wedding before, and he just stood in the back waiting for an eruption. He didn't have to wait long—the bride blew her top when she discovered there was no bride's room in the church and had to get dressed in a public ladies' room. After being in the restroom half an hour doing her makeup and primping, a homeless woman emerged from one of the stalls. She'd apparently just woken up and was delighted to see that there was a bridal party in her midst. "You look nice, missy," she said as she left in time for the lunch in the church's basement soup kitchen. She reappeared in time for the champagne toast; luckily she brought her own cup.

There was another bridal eruption when it was discovered that the expensive wine the bride had selected was not being served, and instead the guests were gagging on lukewarm screw-top wine coolers. Cases of the stuff were left over and spent years after the ceremony sitting in the couple's Toluca Lake, California, garage until the husband donated them to a gay bar next to his office for a benefit carwash. He probably should have told them that they tasted terrible, but he needed the tax deduction.

Another bride with an unlimited budget decided against a photographer and instead hired an avant-garde artist. Unfortunately the painter's day job was as a courtroom sketch artist, and he spent the day profiling felons. When the wedding was over the couple was presented with ten different portraits. In every single one the bride looked guilty, while the groom oddly resembled Robert Blake.

Twenty years later my wife says, "If I'd have known we'd be married this long, I would have had a bigger wedding." But why? You don't need to spend a fortune or hire a professional planner to have a wonderful wedding. On our mantel sits our official wedding-day portrait, where my bride and I are nose to nose standing in a fountain with water up to our knees. We look so young, so happy. The picture was made ten seconds before the four-year-old flower girl socked me where the sun don't shine.

My bride wore a classic strapless white Laura Ashley gown purchased on sale with a coupon just for this day. At the time the cultural zeitgeist was all about **Miami Vice,** so I was marched into the men's department at Bloomingdales where I was instructed to buy an electric blue linen Perry Ellis suit, a pink shirt, pink tie, and pink socks. When my mother saw her only son dressed in a color never worn in Dickinson County, Kansas, she said, "You're so"—She paused to find the exact right word—"bohemian." At first I was insulted, then I rationalized, maybe with all the pink she meant "Bahamian."

The trip into the fountain for the wedding photographer destroyed my brand-new suit; however, for sentimental reasons I kept it hanging in my closet for eighteen years, until my son asked permission to wear it to school. I thought that he wanted it because it was cool looking; in reality they were having a contest for the weirdest article of antique clothing. On the bright side he didn't ask to borrow his mother's wedding dress, but that would have been impossible—it too shrunk and the only person who could possibly fit in it is Malibu Barbie.

But back to that $284 day twenty years ago. I remember sitting inside our Hertz rental car waiting for a thunderstorm to pass before we drove off to our cake soup reception. Aside from our damaged duds, the ceremony had come off without a hitch, and despite the tiny price tag, it was perfect and my bride knew it. At long last, we were finally

Mr. and Mrs. Happy. She turned to me with a smile and said, "I love you."

As her he-man husband of ten minutes, I pulled her close to me and gave her a little kiss. Then I surprised Mrs. Happy with the seven little words few women hear on their wedding day: "I only married you for your kidneys."

GEORGE OF THE WEDDING JUNGLE

W's Dos and Don'ts

We made a few mistakes while planning our wedding. We really should have ordered a tent for an outdoor wedding during tornado season, and as calorie counters we didn't have anybody throw rice because rice is a carb. Why not just hurl a hash brown? If we had it to do all over again, I'm sure we'd ask for help from either a professional wedding planner or maybe a world leader. Don't laugh, I know of one who has a list of dos and don'ts.

The White House is a lot like every other place of employment: when somebody has a baby or gets engaged, the boss finds out quickly.

"The morning after my engagement, which was the morning after his second inaugural," a senior White House official told me, "I went down to the Oval Office and showed him [George W. Bush] my ring. He was very sweet and supportive."

That's when she discovered that her boss, the leader of the free world, not only had a "Road Map for Peace" in the Middle East, he also had an Easy Map to Matrimony. Here are some of the wedding dos and don'ts from America's forty-third president, George W. Bush:

- Have the wedding on a Tuesday, so it can be a low-key affair.
- Have a day wedding—they are less likely to feature dancing (the president is antidancing).
- Keep the mothers out of it, or at least minimize their involvement because they can take over.
- Make it snappy. Don't have a prolonged engagement.

On the last point, she says the president told her, "When you know someone is the one, you just have to move on with it." If you like him, just do it, marry him, and get it over with so you can start your lives together, pronto.

In fact, to save time the president offered her the use of the medical staff at the White House to do the blood test. But she declined, although she could have been the only subscriber to **Modern Bride** magazine who'd had her prewedding tests done by the surgeon general.

During the woman's nine-month engagement the president continued to offer friendly advice regarding her planned September wedding on the island of Mykonos in Greece. He wasn't crazy about their chosen location and wanted her to tear up her game plan. "At one point he was very adamant about us not trying to get legally married in Greece. He could see that it was stressing me out. I was dealing with the Greek embassy, and I was always running to the consulate with a paper."

Then, with the same cut-to-the-chase candor he famously used on Vladimir Putin, Jacques Chiraq, and Tony Blair, he asked, "'Do you really want to marry this guy? If you do, you should do it **now** and do it **here** [in the United States].' And he thought we could go off to Greece for the celebration."

But the young bride felt that if people flew all the way to Greece for a ceremony, she didn't want to cheat them out of the actual wedding. So she stuck to her plan to marry abroad.

The mayor of Mykonos performed the ceremony. "It was all in Greek; only my ninety-five-year-old grandmother understood a word. She loved it. She was blubbering through the whole thing."

The language problem was daunting on their big day, and that official-looking document squirreled away in the "important paper drawer" still haunts her a little. "I'm not certain if I have a title on a car or a marriage license."

So how much of her boss's advice did she take? Let's examine the scorecard.

- Her wedding was not on a Tuesday.
- The mothers were involved in the planning, driving the bride nuts.
- To the president's horror, there was dancing.

In other words, she listened to her boss's advice, nodded as he imparted his wedding wisdom, but in the end, she listened to her heart and had the wedding she'd always dreamed of. That's the way it should be.

The bride always has veto power.

As for the commander-in-chief, I now have a different understanding of the man. Who knew "W" stands for Weddings?

WHAT'S A HONEYMOON?

A History Lesson

We know the honeymoon as the period after the wedding but before the arrival of the first Visa bill.

People have been going on honeymoons for centuries, but only recently have they been close to anything fun, where the bride can order an entrée **and** an appetizer and not get "the stare" from Mr. We're-on-a-Budget.

One legend has it that honeymoons got started in Europe about 300 A.D. The honeymoon would actually take place **before** the marriage. First a man would locate a woman who'd be a suitable wife, but instead of beginning a long and protracted dating period, he would simply abduct her. The man and his friends would then hold the bride hostage until the family forgot that she was missing and moved on to worrying about the birth of the new oxen. Eventually the man would decide it was safe to go home, return triumphantly to announce that they were a couple, then ask his new mother-in-law, "What's for dinner?"

Bride-napping goes back to Attila the Hun, who loved women almost as much as he dug torching villages. So is Attila's moniker, "the Hun," where "**hon**eymoon" comes from?

No.

My research has revealed that during the first month of marriage, the couple would drink a cup of honeyed wine called mead. Just like spring breakers in Fort Lauderdale, the newly married were big drinkers, and they'd have to suck down at least one tumbler every day for the first month, or "moon," of their marriage. Combine the honeyed wine and moon, and you've got "mead-moon." But that doesn't sound like something Jackie

Gleason would ever star in, and early name-makers instead started calling it the honeymoon.

All of this is simply legend. One could always verify part by asking Attila the Hun, but he of course is not available. I believe at this moment he's torching a village in hell.

ADAM AND STEVE

My Accidental Honeymoon

During my single years I was working at an unnamed TV network where I would frequently see Tom Brokaw in the hall. One of my best friends was a videotape editor who suggested we go on vacation together. I'd never been on vacation with a guy other than my dad, who snored through the entire Ring of Kerry.

"Why not!" I told my pal, and he booked the whole thing.

He promised this resort was famous for single girls from Canada, and what better way to show transcontinental hospitality than to buy friendly Canadians an adult beverage or two? That was our plan, but then disaster struck. The day before our flight, the tour company went out of business. My friend had paid with a check, and his money was lost forever. He wasn't going anywhere. I, however, had used the American Express card and was protected. I was suddenly going on vacation solo, but where?

I called a travel agent and asked if she could find me an all-inclusive trip for the next day. Fifteen minutes later she called back. I was booked for Jamaica, which was exciting because I'd never been. And she found a place where everything—drinks, tips, meals, the works—was included in the price. She probably mentioned the name of the resort, but I didn't process it.

The next morning, I was flying Air Jamaica to a week of SPF-300.

At the airport I looked for the bus that would take me to the west end of the island to my resort, Hedonism II. Back then Google did not exist. Too bad, because if I'd have Googled "Hedonism II" I would have discovered I was spending a week at a place referred to as "the Original Party Naked Destination."

When I arrived, people were, thank goodness, wearing clothes—except at one of their two beaches. They had a nude and a prude beach. Let me say under oath and on the record, just in case I'm ever nominated for an associate judgeship on the Supreme Court or **American Idol**, I was proud to be a prude.

When I was escorted to my room, I was surprised to see a suitcase already there. I asked whom it belonged to, and I was told, "Your roommate."

It turns out the only room available twenty-four hours before my arrival was a shared room.

I was naturally expecting the worst, that my roomie would be a Swedish masseuse or Brazilian supermodel. I didn't have to worry about any of that. My roommate was a foot doctor from Michigan. And she was a guy.

Thirty-six hours before we became bunkmates this guy had been standing at the front of a church waiting for his bride to walk down the aisle. She freaked out, then backed out. What are the odds that a foot doctor's fiancée would get cold feet?

They didn't get married. However, he did still have a ticket to Jamaica, and rather than listen to his family hound him for a week asking "What the hell happened?" he called American Express. Just like me, this was the only last-minute resort he could find. So there we were, two total strangers in a double room at the Original Party Naked Destination, during his honeymoon week.

Don't worry, nothing happened—the podiatrist was not my type. I prefer anesthesiologists.

But we did have a great time together. It was the one and only time either of us had ever been at a wet-toga party. Besides, there were buffets brimming with food, plenty of drinks, and great weather. And he found himself very busy, thanks to an occupational benefit of being a bachelor podiatrist at the beach. Girls were constantly wading out into the water, stepping on sea urchins, and then calling for Dr. Scholls (not his real name).

Of course from my training in Kansas, the Beach State, the only treatment I knew of for sea urchin wounds of the foot was to pee on the wound. But I was not a doctor, although I played one on vacation. You know how a foot physician on vacation in Jamaica treats sea urchin stings? He peed on them.

PROS AND CONS OF POPULAR HONEYMOON DESTINATIONS

Location	Pros	Cons
Hawaii	Beautiful, remote, most menus feature raw fish	Very expensive, long trip, most menus feature raw fish
St. Barth's	Great food, lots of celebrities hang out there	Locals speak French and will make fun of your clothes. Also hot French women walk around topless, distracting new husbands

Jamaica	Affordable, tropical, dreadlocks at reasonable rates	Everybody, it seems, is trying to sell you pot; perfect location when Cheech marries Chong
France	Historic, scenic, great food and wine	If they discover you're a Yank, they may give you a swirly
Poconos	Scenic, affordable, convenient to northeast cities	The bathtubs are champagne glasses—don't drink the bathwater
Las Vegas	Bright, brash, something to do all day and night	Gambling is not fun when you lose everything; also, that friendly person in the lobby is a hooker who needs to make a Lexus payment

| Niagara Falls | Stunning, awe-inspiring, Wonder of the World | Constant running water gives you non-stop urge to pee |

LOVERS AND LEPERS

Honeymoon with Meg Ryan

There is no universal "best place" for a honeymoon. Where you go depends upon many things: how much you can spend, what you like to do, and other personal preferences. For ours we flew to the exotic Hawaiian island of Molokai, just a few dozen miles from Maui, which is regarded as the Mount Olympus of honeymoons. We decided to take the island road less traveled.

We'd each been to various Hawaiian Islands before, and at my bride's suggestion we opted for this one because it **sounded** so exotic. There was not one elevator on the island, not one streetlight, and no building taller than a palm tree. Its most famous export is the hula. This place was authentic old Hawaiian.

As we were descending through the scattered clouds after a bumpy seventeen-hour trip from the East Coast, the Air Molokai flight attendant asked us where we were going.

"Molokai."

"Really," she deadpanned. "Why?"

"Because we're traveling on points!"

"Oh," she said, as if she suddenly understood. Then she blitzed us with questions. Where are you staying? Where are you eating? We answered the best we could, until she got to the only question to which I knew the answer for sure. "What are you going to do for a week?"

"Are you kidding?" I said. "We're on our honeymoon." Then I winked at her to drive home the point.

She knew what I meant. "Eventually you'll have to leave the room," she said. "If you get bored, try the leper colony."

Leper colony? As we'd soon learn, an isolated peninsula of the island of Molokai is where thousands of Hawaiians were exiled from society during the last century, because King Kamehameha V (Hawaiian for Larry King) wanted lepers quarantined from the rest of the islands.

"Send them to Molokai," the king declared in 1865.

My new wife had really outdone herself this time. Instead of just booking us onto a cruise that might have an outbreak of the Norwalk virus, or a swanky hotel that had seen a bout of Legionnaires' disease once upon a time, she had found the one spot on earth where not only is clothing optional but apparently so is skin.

As I look back now, years later, I have to laugh. If we had to do it all over again, we would never have planned a honeymoon in Leperville. And here's why. The lepers are in a colony far away from the regular folk. In fact there's not even a paved road that leads you there. But, perhaps because it is the "island of the damned"—my slogan, not the Chamber of Commerce's—there's not a lot going on there.

No air-conditioning, no hair dryers; it's real, it's rustic, it's remote. It's like **Survivor** without the million dollars at the end of the visit. My wife is not into rustic or remote. Her idea of camping is pitching a tent in the lobby of the Ritz-Carlton. We were 5,372 miles from home when it hit me: our honeymoon location was a huge tactical miscalculation on the part of my new wife. And I, the typical rookie husband, didn't let her forget it for one moment.

There was also one early honeymoon howler. I asked our dinner waiter, "What's the mahimahi tonight?"

"The mahimahi is the mahimahi," the 15 percenter replied.

"Au contraire," I started to lecture him. "Mahimahi" was a generic restaurant term much like "soup du jour." Mahimahi, I instructed, meant "fish of the day." I believed that to be true because a real waiter at a nonseafood restaurant in the landlocked state of Kansas told me so. He was wrong, and years later so was I.

"Excuse him, we forgot to pack his medication," my wife apologized to the waiter. Later she insisted I leave him a huge tip, in hopes that he'd not tell the other vacationers that I was suffering from entrée confusion. So just as I didn't let her forget that she'd booked us on a trip to the No Skin Zone, every nine minutes she'd respond to whatever I was talking about with "Oh really,...Mahimahi."

Soon we were barely talking, and then after a few days we were absolutely bored silly. At one point one of us speculated that people here got leprosy (now known as Hansen's disease) just for something to do.

By the final day of our honeymoon we had made up and I pledged that because this had been such a location disaster, we would have a do-over.

Two months later we were off to our second honeymoon.

We ran through National Airport in Washington, D.C., because we'd missed a turn en route and were about to miss our flight to Bermuda. I whipped out our tickets for the gate attendant. I apologized that we were late, I explained the wrong turn, and then I mentioned, "We're going on our honeymoon." The airline girl had been unusually friendly. I figured she was speaking to us as if she knew us because I was a reporter at the NBC station in town, and the Style section of the **Washington Post** had mentioned that we were taking our honeymoon that weekend.

Nope. The agent had glanced at my new wife and thought she was Meg Ryan. Meg Ryan can't be riding in coach! the agent apparently decided. As they held the plane, she scanned a screen, typed something into that clunky computer, and ripped our tickets in half just as the machine under the counter belched out two new boarding passes in first class!

"Have a nice trip, Meg!" she said as we went down the Jetway.

We looked at each other like "What's she smoking?" and didn't know what she was talking about until we plopped down in the first cabin and the flight attendant started laughing.

"What's so funny?" I asked.

"The gate agent thought you're Meg Ryan," she said to my wife.

We all had a good laugh. When we leveled off, the pilot, apparently still under the impression that Meg Ryan was on board, came back to introduce himself. He told us about his time as a Huey pilot in Vietnam, and then added how much he enjoyed my wife in **As the World Turns.** "We have it on in the crew lounge," he added. Then he gave her a pair of wings and returned to flying the plane.

Getting a little buzz from the free American Airlines champagne, I said to my wife, "This honeymoon is already much better than our first, and light-years better than the one with the podiatrist." She nodded her agreement.

Upon arrival we noticed the runway was damp and experienced two to three minutes of glorious dryness before the sheets of rain started banging on the metal roof of the baggage claim. Once again we had not done adequate background checking into our destination, because if we'd asked anybody, they would have told us that we were arriving exactly at the onset of Bermuda's unadvertised monsoon season.

It rained every minute of every day. We were stuck in our bungalow from morning to midnight. The hotel was a perfectly lovely place during the sunny times, but this was not one of them.

"You're kidding," I replied after my wife told me that not a single room at this joint had a television set. "That has got to be against the Geneva Convention." They've got TVs at Alcatraz!

So because of the weather and a Bermuda restriction that American tourists could not rent a car, only a moped, we were shipwrecked indoors. Other than the chance to read (how analog), all we really had to look forward to was the fine dining. Luckily my wife booked us into an inn that specialized in English cuisine. Their specialty was an All-You-Can-Eat Kidney Pie Buffet.

The food was awful, the weather was awful, THERE WAS NO TV, and four days into our do-over honeymoon, we called the airline and booked passage back home to the land of nonvestigial entrées.

The departing gate agent didn't recognize my wife, Meg, and we wound up returning from our Honeymoon in Hell Part Deux in coach.

I still owe the missus three days of honeymooning. But considering our track record, I believe she'll just keep those on account.

We returned home not with sunburns but with windburns.

MRS. HAPPY'S ADVICE

If you find yourself in a bad situation, do your best to fix it. If you can't, be flexible. And if that doesn't work, your only recourse is to laugh. You may be a really good problem solver at work, but on your honeymoon you'll never be able to stop the rain, change a hotel's menu, or cure leprosy.

HONEYMOON HORROR STORY

The Man from Glad

Friends who thought they'd planned their honeymoon perfectly arrived at their remote honeymoon destination only to discover that despite the detailed lists they'd made, the notes they'd taken, and the guidebook they'd followed to the letter, neither brought any sort of family planning protection.

They were desperate, because they were not planning on starting a family that night. The bride, a nurse, knew that any unprotected "relations" would be "a one-way ticket to Pregnant Town."

After a mad search through every piece of their brand-new Eddie Bauer luggage, she finally located in her purse a condom substitute. It was a Baggie. From all reports it worked just fine.

Interestingly, when her husband tells the story, it's a Hefty bag.

PORN TO BE WILD

Should You Camcorder Everything?

So there you are on your honeymoon having the time of your sex lives, when a fragment of an idea hits you…"I've got this new person in my bed, I've got my new camcorder with a remote control, and I've been drinking…Where's my tripod?"

HONEYMOONER ROOKIE MISTAKES

Dos	Don'ts
Visual presentation is important. Any intimate apparel purchased is almost always appreciated by the new spouse.	Don't wear a thong to the pool. Nobody there wants to see your butt.
Be thoughtful and kind to your new spouse.	Spouses never forget mean things said on honeymoons. At all costs avoid the expression "junk in the trunk," even if you're talking about actual junk in your trunk.
During quiet time together, ask your spouse what he/she would like to do.	If you order the hotel porn, you've got an enormous problem that won't be fixed by watching **On Golden Blonde** for $12.95.
Try to make the honeymoon feeling last as long as you can.	Don't steal the sheets as souvenirs—they're dirty. Take the desk.

Thanks to the miracle of Memorex, we know exactly how Tommy Lee and Pamela Anderson spent their honeymoon. And what was Paris Hilton doing in that green grainy video of hers? I heard a rumor that at one point the Paris Hilton video site got more visitors than the Hilton Hotel reservations site.

But what about you? You're not a rocker or hotel heiress. (Attention, Marriott family members reading this, who **are** hotel heirs, please accept my apologies.)

A very famous television personality told me that on several occasions he'd taped himself and his lady. Of course he didn't want those tapes to fall into the wrong hands, and even if they did, he didn't want to be identified, so he'd artfully frame each episode so you couldn't see anybody's face.

He'd watch each tape about a dozen times while she was gone, until the grim reality would set in: "What if I have a heart attack, and somebody goes through my stuff and finds THAT TAPE? Mom just wouldn't get it!"

With that he'd take the tape to the kitchen table and do some careful editing with a twelve-ounce claw hammer. He'd continue to edit until there was nothing left but tiny shards.

Another couple taped their honeymoon "relations." They apparently watched a rerun of their honeymoon fun at least once before vandals stole their VHS player.

Lucky for them, the cops recovered the machine when they busted a local fencing ring. The serial numbers were scratched out, so they really had no way to trace who the owners were, until somebody plugged it in and hooked it to a television. There in grainy green video were the VHS machine's owners. The machine was promptly returned to the high-profile local couple.

Actually it was returned after somebody made a copy of the tape, and reportedly it has been privately shown for years. For years to come this couple would wind up with the longest stares at the Piggly Wiggly, as locals who'd seen the tape would stare and glare.

"Look, Glenn, there's our local porn queen."

"She looks different with her clothes on."

MRS. HAPPY'S ADVICE

To tape or not to tape, that is the question. The answer, simply: No.

Unless your wife is really hot.
Just kidding.

A FOR EFFORT

Grading the Honeymoon

On your trip home, assess the success of your first extended period of time as husband and wife.

While your standards may vary, these are standard measures of success.

GRADE A
- You were inseparable.
- You fell in love a smidgen more.
- You were at a beach and you returned with no tan.

GRADE B
- Nobody gained weight.
- A good time was had by all.
- You used a five-dollar-off coupon for the glass-bottomed boat tour.

GRADE C
- You had a major argument over the cost of the souvenir ukulele.
- Somebody fell asleep the first night and could not be awakened.
- One spouse was on the phone in the first three days with her/his mother: "Yeah, yeah, yeah, you told me so…"

GRADE D
- The box of protection devices was unopened.
- The box of Pepcid AC was entirely consumed.

GRADE F

- You argued all the way from the wedding reception through the entire honeymoon.
- One spouse slept with a member of the housekeeping or landscaping staff.
- There was gunplay.

chapter three

Marriage

YOU'RE MR. & MRS. HAPPY

Now What?

With one "I do" you've gone from Lean Cuisine singles to the KFC Family Pack.

You're now entering an exciting time of change and transformation.

Ladies, marriage is something many of you have been training and waiting for your whole life. Those hours spent in high school study hall idly doodling your future married name—"Sincerely, Mr. and Mrs. Anderson Fabulous"—have finally paid off.

Guys, many of you are very macho dudes who believe that you'll always be 180 pounds of "twisted steel and sex appeal." However, thanks to the miracle of marriage, you're about to change, big-time. Chances are, by your third anniversary, you'll be walking three paces behind your wife through the mall, carrying her purse. And will you be worried what other guys think? Heck no. You'll be mortified that her bag doesn't match your shoes.

It's just the cost of admission to a lifetime with someone who will not only make life worth living but who you can talk to forever, which is especially important when the power goes out.

One morsel of advice, guys: if she relocates to your bachelor cave, let her change anything she wants. Curtains, bedspreads, kitchen appliances, whatever. Do you really care if you get the twelve-cup Cuisinart coffeemaker in brushed steel instead of matte black metal? Of course not. But you do have a demand. Just one.

She cannot under any circumstances disconnect your cable or Internet.

We all have our Alamos.

TIME LINE OF FIRST MARRIAGE

200,000 years ago
God creates Adam.

↓

God borrows rib,
creates Eve.

↓

Adam appreciates having female companionship,
asks her to "make me a sandwich."

↓

Mating dance simple,
she is the only woman on earth.

↓

Not surprisingly,
Adam and Eve have children,
Cain, Abel, Seth.

↓

Life is paradise, until…
Cain kills Abel.
Seth is never indicted.

↓

Satan (serpent) tempts Eve with forbidden fruit.
Eve bites, assured by serpent the apple
has no trans fats.
Eve invents takeout and takes forbidden
fruit home to Adam.

↓

Adam and Eve have forbidden-fruit picnic.

↓

Big mistake; they blame everybody but O.J.

↓

Adam and Eve are evicted by God from the
Garden of Eden.

↓

Adam and Eve wander aimlessly; Adam is too
embarrassed to ask for directions.

WHAT WE REALLY WANT

The Lowdown on Love

Wives want someone who'll look at the VISA bill and say, "Is that all you spent this month? Next month go crazy!" and mean it. They want someone who'll hold their hand and comfort them when their favorite is voted off **American Idol.** Women want a solid guy who'll say, "You look pretty and smell good," and really mean it.

Husbands want a 50-inch plasma screen.

I CAN SEE CLEARLY NOW

The End of the Honeymoon Effect

You're picking up a weird vibe. You're already halfway through a roll of Tums, and they're not working. They said it would happen, but you thought you'd be different, you'd have that "just married" feeling FOREVER! Maybe it started when your goofball new spouse tried to shove cake in your piehole.

Up till now, you've been HUI, or honeymooners under the influence. If only a couples cop would pull you over when he suspects your condition and ask for license and registration (marriage license and bridal registration). Then in that "just the facts, ma'am" cop voice he'd explain the honeymoon effect.

"It's that misty, wonderful, warm and gooey feeling after the wedding when everything is beautiful," the cop explains. "When you love being in love, blah blah blah…whatever."

Then he would administer a Breathalyzer, to see how close you are to sobering up. And how long until you start calling a spade a shovel. Unfortunately the Breathalyzer flashes a large number that means you've apparently also just consumed half a dozen Schlitzes, but that's okay, because he's not a real cop. I'm making this up!

Of course I'm not a cop either, although I do have a set of handcuffs. Don't ask. But ladies and gentlemen, don't be depressed about the honeymoon effect coming to an end. This is when it starts getting good.

FROM "I DO" TO "UH-OH"

Retraining the New Hire

You're back from the honeymoon. In the freezer of your newly acquired KitchenAid side-by-side refrigerator is the surviving top tier of wedding cake, just under the Mrs. Paul's Beer Battered Fish Fillets.

You feel you're off to a solid start as man and wife. However, slowly you start to notice important details about the person you just married, details that you've previously glossed over.

- "When she said she's a vegan, I thought that meant she was from Vegas."
- "I thought he had a pole installed in the bedroom because his fantasy was to be a fireman! But he's just an auto-parts salesman who loves strippers!"

Those cracks in the façade—maybe it's buyer's remorse, whatever, it happens to us all. It's known as PWSS, or post-wedding shockers syndrome.

When I was growing up in Kansas, I had a neighbor who waited until he was in his mid-thirties to marry. He was a good man and a hard worker. He finally surprised us all when he asked a beautiful blonde to be his bride. It was also a surprise that she, a city girl, would marry him, because life on the farm takes some adjusting.

Farmhouses don't have the luxury of a sewer system, relying instead upon a septic tank, just like millions of other American homes. The new groom was a crackerjack farmer but didn't quite understand the physics of the septic process—he thought that any paper flushed down the toilet would go into the tank and clog it up. That was the last thing he wanted, especially during harvest. So he had a house rule that nobody could ever flush any paper products down the potty. No newspapers, Sears or Spiegel catalogs, no utility bills. And no toilet paper.

After their honeymoon in Branson and Silver Dollar City, he carried his new bride over the threshold into their love nest, then explained to her that from this day forward, she would never flush toilet paper down the toilet. She was instructed to use the Charmin for her "personal business" and then place it in a trash can near the toilet. Then every couple of days the groom would take it out back and burn it, much to the delight of downwind neighbors—us.

My new wife was oblivious to my mortal side, never seeming to notice any of my foibles; she loved being married. During the first year she'd wake me in the middle of the night to say hi. She smiled all the time. She laughed at all of my bad jokes. And—this was a killer—she used to take a steak knife and trim the crust from my tuna sandwich to shape it like a heart. No wonder my tuna tasted like ventricle.

I was the first one who got that misty honeymooner sentimentality out of my bloodstream. Don't get me wrong, I loved being married. But when you're first "in love" and going through the process of planning a wedding and the honeymoon and whatnot, you overlook some things. I don't know how I missed it the first five hundred meals we had together, but during a Saturday brunch somewhere as my wife was talking, I noticed that every time she was about to take a bite of her food, she would first move a piece of salad, or touch something on her plate with her fork, exactly eleven times. Not ten times, not twelve times, but eleven times.

Like the cop watching the perp through the one-way glass in the interrogation room, I watched her for the entire meal. One, two, three, four, five, six, seven, eight, nine, ten, and on eleven she'd fork something and down the hatch it would go. For some unknown reason, she needed to build up to the bite, the culinary climax, making those first ten touches; it was like food foreplay.

I found this shocking. She's the most beautiful woman I'd ever met, perfect in every way...I'd thought. But I just realized, "My wife's not a calorie counter, she's Rain Man!"

"One, two, three, four, five, six, seven, eight, nine, ten, eleven. Eleven minutes, to Wapner."

When I pointed out this dining discovery, as soon as the words left my lips I realized I'd hurt her feelings, and suddenly I felt terrible. She, on the other hand, tried to take the high road and prove she was no Pavlov's wife. She stabbed an avocado on the first try, clearly visualizing it as my head, but that's something she's going to have to work out next time she phones in to Dr. Laura. A desperate phone call to a radio-show WATS line is generally a good sign that the honeymoon is over. Now the only number crunching I do while dining out is figuring out the tip.

A couple I know who'd spent a romantic engagement living on different continents had some major adjusting to do when they finally moved into her eleven-hundred-square-foot Manhattan apartment. Giddy playing the new wife, she wanted to please her man, so she surprised him by happily doing his laundry and putting it in "his side" of the dresser. Then she proudly called him in to examine her handiwork. There was a pained expression on his face as he opened each drawer. But he said not a word. Disappointed that he'd not lavished her with some compliment, she left. When she returned that night she wanted to take one more look at the good job she'd done and was shocked to see that he'd taken everything out of the bureau and rearranged it.

"He didn't like the way I'd folded things. He had exact places on his clothes where he wanted creases; I didn't know where they were." They immediately struck a deal; from that day forward, he would do the laundry. However, there was another crack in the façade at feeding time: "His food must be lined up a certain way on the plate," she explained. "The asparagus has to be pointing due east, or he can't eat it." His plate is laid out like a map; it's the Food Network meets the Discovery Channel.

Despite the oddities, she's fine with whatever he wants to do. So what if he's a little obsessive-compulsive? She said he's a "good kisser," which is more important than how he "folds his damned Dockers."

MR. HAPPY'S ADVICE

It's a good thing that honeymoon feeling doesn't last forever.

Newlyweds gloss over real problems and never address them because they don't want to rock the boat. That's not a terrific way to have an honest relationship. But eventually both sides snap out of it. Then they enter the phase where that fleeting, goofy, inexplicable feeling of just-got-hitched love is replaced by real love.

Meanwhile, back to my wife the food counter, she still does it. Occasionally over dinner I'll start the tote board in my head, and as soon as the Countess Von Count realizes I'm tallying her tallying, she gives me that "I should have married that cute dentist!" look.

Actually, when I get the dentist bill for her and our three orthodontically perfect kids, I sometimes wish the same thing.

WEDDING CAHER

I Married a Cheapskate

"My husband's mother had just passed away after a long illness," the wife began, recounting the day her husband and his siblings finished the grim task of making his mother's funeral arrangements.

"All right, I think we've got all we need," announced the funeral director, "now if you'll follow me to the Slumber Room," and like dazed sheep, they followed the man in black.

"Please take your time deciding upon a casket for your mother," he said, and headed into the soft-sell pitch he'd perfected during the last twenty-three years in the funeral-parlor business. That's when the deceased mother's firstborn interrupted.

"Oh, we already bought a coffin. And we're having it sent over this afternoon."

The undertaker stopped, stunned. "When did you make those arrangements?"

"Last week. We knew she was close to the end."

"Where?"

"Direct Casket, Van Nuys."

Suddenly the funeral-director-turned-Monty-Hall tried to make a deal. "I wish you'd have given me the opportunity to meet their price."

"Look," the son said, "we remember how we got stung by you when Dad died."

"I see," said Mr. End of the Trail. And with that they made a left from the Slumber Room to visit the office manager and write a check for one funeral, sans box.

Could you put Momma in a wholesale casket?

(Voice from the Great Beyond: "Seven years of breast-feeding, and **this** is my thanks?")

You'd think that Mr. Thrift doesn't have much money. That would be incorrect. His family is loaded. They just hate to spend the dough, and it drives his wife nuts. Here are a few more examples:

- His family drives a fleet of high-line luxury cars (Mercedeses, Range Rovers, and Lexuses), and yet they won't valet park. Their official reason? "Somebody'll look in the glove compartment, see where we live, and rob us!" "That's a lie," his wife said. "They just don't want to tip the valet a dollar."

- At bath time, he'll put just two inches of cold water in the tub, to save on his gas bill. His wife fills it to the brim with scalding water and then lets it cool down before she gets in. That really fries his calamari.

- He won't let his wife see their joint tax return because he doesn't want her to know how much money he makes. She has learned the hard way that signing a 1040 with a blindfold is guaranteed to smear your makeup.

The husband also refuses to call a skilled craftsman when a home emergency occurs. The wife will inject over breakfast, "The toilet won't stop running."

"I'll fix it as soon as I get home tonight," he says, apparently making a mental note.

Of course he's said he'd fix it as soon as he gets home tonight for the last four mornings. So one day while he's at work, she calls a plumber, who comes and fixes it. When the bill arrives in a week or two, she'll hide it, because he'd hit the roof if he found out another man was in the house laying hands on his wife's pipes.

Cheapness aside, she really loves him. "He's a terrific father, and a good husband." And despite the cold-water baths, the wholesale coffin, and the stealth plumber visits, she knows he has a special place in his heart for her.

"Nothing says I love you more than knowing he'll be going to the 99¢ Only store at five o'clock on Mother's Day."

LOVE ME (LEGAL) TENDER

Marrieds and Money

I am the son of Depression-era parents. I have spent the last forty-some-odd years going through our house turning off the lights to save money. Meanwhile, my wife is a spender. It wouldn't shock me to go home and hear that she's hired a private tutor to teach our golden retriever to speak Dutch.

I have a sophisticated sniffer when it comes to WMD (women, men, dollars).

There are three possible husband/wife combinations:

- Both are spenders. (Good thing they have overdraft protection.)
- Both are savers. (One still has the ten-dollar check Grandma sent as a nineteenth-birthday present.)
- A spender is married to a saver. (The spender thinks the saver is a tightwad, and the saver thinks the spender incorrectly assumes they're married to an Onassis.)

When both are on the same financial page, great. But when a saver marries a spender, trouble usually follows quickly.

A woman (spender) told me a story about how she was able to convince her husband (saver) that she was saving tons of money, while in fact she was bleeding the family's piggy bank dry. (Attention, organized-crime-family-members: Take notes; this has potential.)

He loved her completely, despite the fact that she was a shopaholic. It got to the stage where at the end of the month they had to decide who'd get paid—the electric company or Neiman Marcus. (She chose Neiman's, reasoning that if she was going to be sitting in total darkness after they cut the power to their home, she really must have sheets with an astronomical thread count.)

Finally he was on the verge of issuing food vouchers. "Stop spending so much," he told her, "or I'm going to start handling all financial transactions."

Well, the last thing she wanted was to be on an allowance. Not that month—Bloomingdale's was having a white sale. Psychologists say shopaholics can't change overnight. The urge to splurge is very powerful. And you know the old expression, "When the going gets tough, the tough go shopping." So she did.

At the mall, she continued on her buying binge. Whatever she wanted, she bought. Because she had a plan. One so foolproof that her room-temperature-IQ-husband would never figure it out.

At the conclusion of her retail mission, she set up shop in the parking garage. She took all of her new acquisitions from her shopping bags and placed them next to her on the passenger seat. Then she opened a brand-new red Flair pen fresh off the shelves of Staples.

It was time to put her plan in motion.

She held in her hands a beautiful Eileen Fisher blouse; the tag read $110, which she had just paid at Nordstrom. She took her Flair, crossed out the $110, and scribbled a big red $55, just like stores do when they put something on the markdown rack.

Thanks to her red pen she was able to **edit** the prices of all of her purchases. Genius.

"How much was that?" he'd ask when he came home, and she'd cheerfully whip out the tag, which was Exhibit A.

"Look, it was half price!" she'd say, beaming.

How could he be mad at his wife if she was saving so much on each and every item? Not only that, he thought he'd really made an impact on her, since she was apparently only shopping the clearance aisle.

Of course nothing could be further from the truth. Maybe I've seen too many episodes of **Law & Order,** but why didn't he ever ask why Old Navy, Ann Taylor, and the Gap all have sales prices in the same red ink **and** the same handwriting? And why didn't he ask to see the actual receipt?

Simple—he was desperate to believe that she'd changed, and when she said she had, and showed him her "markdowns," it was enough proof for him.

"Thanks, Hot Stuff, you're the best."

When I regaled my wife with that story, her eyes opened wide as she drank in every detail. Nodding, she had a one-word assessment of the Flair scam: "Brilliant." When I asked her whether **she** laundered money, she gave me that same pained look a person gets when asked to be a bone-marrow donor.

My wife was a big spender; when we first got married, she spent money like she was printing it at Kinko's, which at that time was illegal. When we were on vacation and she wasn't at the malls, Greenspan would call and ask if everything was all right. She called it "retail therapy," which, she reminded me, was "cheaper than a funeral."

During our first ten years of marriage, I did my best to redirect her shopping. I took her to big-box stores and wholesale places, where she learned that buying in bulk was fun. And that she could not only shop, she could shop with a forklift! "I never wore a hard hat at Macy's!" she squealed with delight.

She got to the point where she was buying so much stuff in vast quantities, she traded her Rabbit cabriolet for a Volvo station wagon. She needed towing capacity. My wife declined to be interviewed on this topic for this book and referred me to her lawyer. Which was interesting, because we don't have a lawyer.

Meanwhile, I'm tighter than the rusted lug nuts on a '65 Chevy. However, she still loves a bargain, like when I got home and noticed something new in the driveway.

"Where did you get the helicopter?" I inquired.

"Homeland Security," she responded. "And I used a coupon."

I probably should have asked more questions, but we're now the first ones on the block with a Sikorski, and I know that really bothers our neighbor with the Mercedes.

MRS. HAPPY'S ADVICE

In the beginning, set limits. "This is how much we can spend." Period.

There will be times when one party overspends. Just adjust. The next month, there will be some belt tightening. Establish cause and affect. "Just 'cause you wanted this, it will affect your new bath-oil purchase."

And a note to you cheapskates from somebody who is married to Mr. Thrifty. The life of a miser is a lonely one. Why are you saving? For retirement with that person you just berated for buying a four-dollar café mocha latte? Four bucks, big deal. When you're retired, you can go to the early-bird special and save five—the cost of that coffee drink. There is something called Quality of Life. So don't make a big deal when your spouse occasionally buys something that makes her feel good. Life is short. Even if the time until the next Diners Club bill comes is shorter.

Finally, I suggest that when in public places like malls and superstores, you always hold hands. It reminds your one and only that you love her. Also if you let go, she'll shop.

TASTES LIKE CHICKEN

The Fear Factor

Todd is a good man. A fine father. A good provider. But he's a big baby. Early in his marriage he needed a blood test to check his blood type. It was a fertility thing. He wanted to start a family, but "No way" was he rolling up his sleeve for his wife. Why?

As a boy, Todd severely cut his finger. The gushing blood so scared him that he passed out.

At the hospital, when he saw the needle for the tetanus shot, he passed out. He came to just as they were giving him a Novocain shot, which caused him to faint a third time. And when he opened his eyes, he saw them stitching him up, and of course, this towering mountain of a man blacked out an impressive fourth time.

From that day forward, no needle would ever puncture any part of him. That meant that years later, if somebody had to spill blood to start a family, it would have to be his wife. She got tested, and she wasn't the problem; the doctor needed Todd's blood. But he was clear: "Absolutely not!"

So his beautiful wife, Madeline, did what any desperate housewife who just happened to be a nurse would do. She woke up at four-thirty one morning, squirted some alcohol on his arm, tapped out a vein, stuck in a needle, and drew out the blood. WHILE HE WAS ASLEEP.

He didn't feel a thing, but it made me worry. If she can do that to her sleeping husband, what could other wives do to theirs? "Honey, have you seen my spleen?" says the man pointing to his spleen department. "It was right here when I went to bed."

I love Madeline's ingenuity. Also, despite the fact that she's a female, she's a true Boy Scout in the "Be prepared" department. In her glove compartment she has an umbilical-cord clamp and a bulb syringe, just in case she has to deliver a baby while stuck in traffic. That explains the vinyl seats.

As for the middle-of-the-night blood vial, first thing in the morning she whisked it off to the lab, where the doctor ran some tests. But before any fertility treatment was started, she got pregnant the old-fashioned way. So I guess he's not **that** girly.

I suffer from the same thing Todd has, and chances are my fellow husband readers do too; fear of **any** medical procedure. Needles, IVs, suppositories, and of course, the big kahuna to anyone over forty, the colonoscopy. Just at the mention of any of them I get that same sharp pain in the gut that Superman would feel when somebody had Kryptonite nearby.

The funny thing is, none of those things bug most wives.

That's because as the child-bearing genders, they routinely have every intimate part prodded, poked, and pulverized by somebody with cold hands and coffee breath. Back in the day, women would squat in a field, deliver a baby, then finish bringing in the crop. Only afterward would they tend to the baby in the bushel basket and say, "I think I'll name him Milo."

MR. HAPPY'S ADVICE

Just accept the fact that men and women are afraid of different things.

And that's okay. But it begs the question, if husbands go wobbly on almost all important health issues, why should women stay married to squirmy good-for-nothing guys?

That's easy.

About once a month, Todd will get a shrieking cell phone call from his normally stoic wife. "Come home NOOOOWWW!!!" Click.

He'll race home, find her screaming like a woman, scan the room, roll up a magazine, cock his arm, and fire away, instantly squashing the scary bug with thirty-seven hairy legs, leaving a little gut trail that he'll mop up with the back of the hand holding a doughnut.

"That's why I married him," she boasts of her one-man Orkin army.

Husbands. I's not much, but it's all we have.

THE EDIT SWEET

Honesty

It was supposed to be a fun night with the neighbors; we were playing the "Not-So-Newlywed Game." Because Bob Eubanks was busy, I was the host. I still remember the answer that stopped the night.

"Gentlemen, where would you like to see a picture of your wife…"

That's a loaded question. But then again, so was the crowd.

"Where would I like to see a picture of my wife?" one of my neighbors repeated. "At her wake!"

The room went silent. The only sound heard was the hum of the rented Mr. Margarita machine.

Generally a person has to be embedded with a family for years before that kind of honesty is displayed in public. Most happy couples I know use what I call selective honesty. Some things you can be honest about, but others you must **edit**.

Sadly, it's hard to edit when you're drunk.

We were at a friend's landmark birthday party, late one evening, and I found myself in the kitchen wedged between two couples with whom I'm friendly. They'd started drinking at lunch, and I was still on my first spritzer, so I did my best to translate the slurred speech. I picked up quickly that in high school the wife of one couple had dated the husband of the other.

"Do you remember the time," the one wife said to her former boyfriend, "that you took me to the homecoming dance and then you #%$ed me?"

The husband nodded as their distant one-nighter haunted him in front of his current wife and her lucky husband.

"You were the worst I ever had," she spat.

Defending her husband's honor, the other wife snapped, "You tell that story every time you drink cosmos. You're a drunk and a slut."

"I **was** a slut," the cosmo drinker said. "Now I'm just a drunk."

Her husband nodded. "She's a drunk." He was on his fifth martini. They had a marriage made in Absolut heaven.

There are so many things wrong with their boozy dialog. At least one of them needed to be doing some selective editing. But it's hard to regulate what gems tumble out of your mouth when you've got the blood-alcohol level of turpentine.

Today my wife and I are completely evolved in the honesty department. When she asks for the truth, she knows that if it's hurtful, I'll edit my response. So the only way for her to get the "true" truth requires three shots of Demerol.

Being a man in his late forties, I'd been **thinking** about getting a colonoscopy someday, but I hadn't advanced much, until a friend had his life saved with one. So I scheduled a visit to Dr. Rooter.

This was a landmark trip to the hospital for me. I'd never had an IV, never gotten one of those plastic wristbands, nothing. So in many ways, I was a virgin until my first colonoscopy. (Author's note: **Virgin** and **colonoscopy** scare men when used in the same sentence; please edit out for paperback version.)

Once I was wheeled into the exam room, I engaged in probably twenty-seven seconds of small talk with the nurse before she squirted three consecutive doses of Demerol into my IV and I was off to see the wizard.

Thirty minutes later when I woke up, the doctor told me, "You're fine, no complications."

Then he told me that the exam wasn't nearly as tough as the grilling I got when I returned to the recovery area.

"Whaddya meaaan?" I slurred in that way you do when you've had too many drinks but you're trying to act like you're stone-cold sober.

"Ask your wife about the cross-examination."

"WHHHAAADD? She was in there?" (Never ask a colonoscopy guy who **else** was "in there.")

As I later reconstructed the time line, after the procedure the nurse brought my wife to see me, and I was still in that chatty altered state known as the "spilling your guts zone."

Realizing this was her chance to get the **true** truth for perhaps the first time in our marriage, my wife the amateur lie-detector examiner started to question me, beginning with a "control question" to see if I was truthful.

"Did you like that pesto I made two nights ago?"

Without the benefit of my editing gene turned on, I responded with an honest "It tasted like crap." She reported that I said, "You forgot the pine nuts. I hate it when the pine nuts go bye-bye."

With a truth baseline established, she moved on to topic A. "When was the last time you had an affair?"

Defenseless, I started to laugh.

"When?"

More giggling.

"Have you ever had an affair?" she pressed.

Then, she reported, I turned and looked at her, and with one eye on hers and the other rolling around in the back of my head, I cooed, "Nope. Never. I love **youuuuuuu**." Then I gurgled and fell fast asleep.

A relieved nurse who witnessed the cross-examination said that she sees husbands and wives ask their spouses those questions all the time. It was, however, the first time she said she'd heard "pine nuts" in the colonoscopy suite. I'm glad.

MARRIED TO THE MOM

In-laws

Two weeks before her wedding, a Phoenix woman and her fiancé had one final dinner with her soon-to-be in-laws. They were strict Roman Catholics and were spending extra time praying the rosary in hopes that their son would not marry this woman, who was not only Protestant but divorced.

They had attempted over the previous few weeks to get her to sign a prenup that would give her husband everything **she** had if they ever broke up. There had never been a divorce in their family, and they wanted to lock her up with platinum handcuffs so that she would stay married. They were doing everything they could to make sure there would not be a divorce on their watch.

She wouldn't bend from their badgering, and when they demanded she sign on the line, she simply said, No.

This meal was one final chance to smoke the peace pipe before the wedding. As the dinner wound down, the future bride excused herself to the ladies' room. After returning to the table five minutes later, she immediately felt an awkwardness she hadn't noticed before. It was hard to miss—nobody was talking. Instead they pushed their cheesecake around their plates and guzzled coffee that the waiter had promised was decaf. After four or five painful minutes of radio silence, the father started to speak.

"I jus—"

Instantly his wife barked, "Shut up and eat."

A few minutes later her fiancé announced, "We're done with dinner," and they exited the restaurant, leaving his pushy parents with the bill.

"What happened?" the future bride asked. He reported that when she had gone to the ladies' room, his mother had pulled out a contract. It was not the prenup they'd hounded her to sign—this was a contract just for him. Prepared by the family's lawyers, it was quite simple. If their son agreed **not** to marry the girl in the restroom, they would pay him one million dollars.

Of course a young man in love can always find a love loophole, so they closed a big one; in case he canceled the wedding but lived with her, no jackpot either. The contract specified that he could also never **see** her again.

He added, "Don't worry, I'm not signing. We're getting married."

Horrified, she paused to take it all in: her future mother-in-law had essentially put out a contract on her. If he just whacked the wedding and steered clear of her, he'd have one million reasons to smile.

One million is a lot of money. That's when she realized, "They should have offered **me** the contract!"

Two weeks later they got married; her new in-laws were no-shows.

On their honeymoon she suddenly took ill. She'd contracted a weird strain of a deadly disease that short-circuited their honeymoon, sending her into the infectious-disease ward of a big metropolitan hospital. The new couple was faced with the real danger that she would die.

You've got to figure the groom was probably thinking, "She might die—maybe I should have taken that million after all…"

But she pulled through.

When she was well enough to go home, her husband, who had been with her through it all, opened a Pandora's box and whispered that he thought her illness had not been accidentally contracted on their wedding trip. He speculated that as a last resort, his mother had poisoned her that night at dinner.

It turns out the incubation period for her particular disease is two weeks. And two weeks before she got sick, she'd been in a restaurant restroom reapplying her lipstick as her future mother-in-law tried to buy off her boy.

Coincidence? You be the judge.

Suddenly your in-law stories seem so petty. When was the last time your mother-in-law tried to rub you out?

MRS. HAPPY'S ADVICE

In-laws are great. At a distance. Mine have always been approximately three thousand miles away. If they ever try

to sneak across the country to visit, thanks to friends at **NORAD**, as soon as they cross the Mississippi a red light flashes on my desk and we quickly pack up and head to the Poconos.

You, however, may live within shouting distance of your in-laws. I know people who live in the same town, some on the same street, some in the same house. There is a special place in heaven waiting for all of them.

There are a few things that are universal when it comes to in-laws.

1. You were not **their** first choice to be their child's spouse.
2. They would like you to listen to their advice once in a while.
3. Odds are, they will die before you, and if you keep in mind there is a large estate waiting for some of you one day, you'll realize it doesn't pay to fight with them, so shut up and smile.

You must find a way to get along. Otherwise you are doomed to a lifetime of popping Tums.

The in-law conundrum is one you will struggle with your entire married life. When you got hitched, you knew you'd be adopting your spouse's family, you just didn't realize they were the Addams Family.

I DROPPED WHEN I SHOPPED

Gift Fatigue

Every spring I develop what mallologists refer to as "gift fatigue." I lose the will to buy.

That's because over twelve days in May, I have to buy my wife gifts for her birthday, our anniversary, and Mother's Day. (Note to Hallmark: If it's Mother's Day, shouldn't the gifts come from the kids? I'd be happy to get her something for Wife's Day, especially since it doesn't exist.)

Real men don't shop; they buy, and buy fast.

It is a well-known fact that the busiest day women shop is the day after Thanksgiving. The busiest shopping day for men is Christmas Eve. Why is that? Probably because men are practical, beer-driven individuals who don't like to waste a lot of time, especially at a mall, where ESPN reception is iffy.

My friend Mike is just like me, except of course he's taller, smarter, and more successful. I admire him greatly. Especially in light of one pre-Santa performance that is still legend in his home state. It was Christmas Eve, and around noon, Mike went to the mall for his annual visit. He apparently had done some planning, and was able to locate the gift item he desired and return to his car in an impressive twenty minutes. He'd achieved the Holy Grail of Giftery. He'd purchased his wife a spectacular sapphire-and-diamond ring that would make her weep with joy. And the best part—it took less than half an hour.

When his wife, Judy, opened it up, she couldn't believe it. "I LOVE this!" she exclaimed.

The year before, Mike's intimate gift to his wife of twenty years had been the always romantic twenty-four-piece Tupperware Classic Collection. The ring made up for a lifetime of bad gifts.

Judy kept looking at him, and then the ring, and then back at him, and proudly declared, "This is why I married you. You know what I want!"

Mike spent the next year in the rarified aura of Best Husband in the Neighborhood. For me, as a man, he was tough to live next to. Fast-forward to the next Christmas. Naturally Judy, and the other neighborhood wives, wanted to know how Mike would top last year's jackpot.

Beaming, he presented her with another little black box.

"It's not a fishing pole." She knew what it was: another piece of jewelry!

She popped the lid open and laid her eyes upon this year's gift. She was stunned. It was spectacular. It was dazzling. It was exactly the same sapphire-and-diamond ring he'd given her the year before.

At first she thought he'd wrapped up last year's gift as a joke, until she looked at her right hand, and parked there was the original.

"I thought it looked familiar!" he explained through the suddenly locked bedroom door.

Personally, I hate the mall, even though I can be in and out in less than fifteen minutes. That is possible because just like Mike, I always buy the woman I love the same thing.

Last year it was a brown Kate Spade Pia purse for $145. This year it was a pink Kate Spade Pia purse for $145 for her birthday, and a black Pia for Mother's Day. The day after her birthday, she'll return it like the many that came before it.

My wife, on the other hand, always gets me thoughtful and practical stuff. My only requirement is that whatever it is, it should be cheap. I've already got everything I need, so whatever she buys I really don't need, and we both know it.

Men struggle with gifts for women, and yet women seem so good at buying an appropriate gift for their guys.

Actually, men are just better actors than women. When we open the box and see the bottle of Kouros by YSL and a stupid necktie covered with galloping ponies, we have the same reaction: "Thank you! This is great! I really love it!" In reality what men really want is a new plasma-screen television where the Playboy Channel mysteriously appears each Friday and Saturday night, fifteen minutes after the kids go to bed.

But that's not going to happen. So in the real world, where the man is just grateful that she's still with him after years of him leaving the toilet seat up, he'll happily accept **anything** and like it.

"Ponies! How'd you know I love ponies?"

MR. HAPPY'S ADVICE

Never buy a woman an appliance. Unless Ralph Lauren makes a toaster oven, put it back. A household device subliminally says, "Happy anniversary, honey. Now get in the kitchen and make me a corn dog." In other words, if a gift plugs in, you won't.

Also, clotheswise, always buy size small.

Once I bought my wife a winter coat for Christmas. I didn't want to ask her what size she was in a coat, because I didn't want to tip her off. It was really nice, and it looked like it was about her size.

So I got her an 18.

Turns out it was eight sizes too big.

She did not speak to me, except through the children, until Valentine's Day.

"Tell your father Cupid is dead."

SATURDAY-NIGHT FIGHTS

How to Argue Without Gunplay

There will come a time when you disagree about something really important.

> "Who was that guy in Full Metal Jacket?"
> he asked his wife. "Ethan Some-
> body."
> "You're thinking of Matthew Modine!"
> she replied.
> "Hawke...Ethan Hawke."
> "I just saw it on Cinemax; it was Mat-
> thew Modine."
> "Twenty bucks says you're wrong."
> "Twenty bucks says you're an idiot!"
> "I never loved you."
> (Momentary pause for drama)
> "And one more thing. Your mother's
> meat loaf tastes like tree bark!"

The International Court of Justice in The Hague would rule that that comment was totally uncalled-for, even if that bite was worse than the mother's bark.

There are a few things you should never do when arguing:

- Name-call (they get that at work)
- Have liquor on your breath
- Yell
- Make stuff up
- Say stuff that leaves a mark
- Insult your spouse's mother's comfort foods

Survival of the fittest is clear; if you're in a fight, you should fight to win. However, this is not Ali versus Frazier, it's you versus your loved one. Here's the problem with fighting dirty. We all keep tucked away in our heads a file of embarrassingly hideous mistakes our spouse has made throughout history. As soon as we whip out one of those gems, all bets are off. That argument will disintegrate into name-calling, hurt feelings, and torrents of tears. Think Hannity & Colmes, with streaked mascara.

If in the heat of an argument you deploy one of those neutron bombs, where the furniture is still intact but all lives are lost, you can stick a fork in your relationship because it's dead for months, even years. You may never be forgiven for bringing up an item of such lethal proportions. Not even a month of renting Nora Ephron films will get you out of the doghouse.

If you're negotiating at the United Nations or a new contract for the United Auto Workers, then by all means go for the jugular. But I have discovered after twenty years of arguing, I don't have to win every time. I intend to live with this woman until I'm at the all-Jell-O-every-meal stage.

So I have compromised. I have a new, relaxed approach to arguing. In the beginning, I just make sure that my wife hears what I have to say. So I'll say it a couple of times. If she doesn't bite, I don't jam it down her throat.

Also, now I listen. Once upon a time, I argued willy-nilly, gladiator-style, beating my opponent to a bloody pulp, without realizing on rare occasions that my opponent was right. Now I listen. And if my wife is right, I'll admit it.

Keep in mind this is a very evolved way of thinking. It took me many years to realize that sometimes it's not worth three months of getting frozen out on Friday nights, just to argue over whether you're supposed to put paprika on the top of potato salad. Which is an argument we've had twice a year for twenty summers. My wife says no. I say yes because it's the way my mother made it. And Mom is always right.

As an evolved spouse, I know the paprika question is not something that I need to develop an aneurysm over. Argue over big things, not details. A reddish spice is not worth wasting a valuable chit. Since my wife makes the potato salad, it's her call; she can make it any way she wants. In my head I'll **know** it would taste 25 percent better peppered with paprika, but instead I quietly eat in silent desperation.

MRS. HAPPY'S ADVICE

NASCAR superstar Dale Jarrett said the key to arguing is "never go to bed without settling your argument." The Oscar-winning actress Olympia Dukakis echoed his point. Once you find yourself tangled in a troublesome argument, you have to "stay in the room," she advised. That makes perfect sense. If the husband and wife stay in the room until they've talked over their differences and ironed out a solution, they'll never leave angry. Just "duke it out" and "don't leave until you see the other side," she added. Once again correct. No wonder she's an award winner.

Of course had Olympia personally "stayed in the room," her Oscar would not have been stolen. She appeared on a television program and the host asked her where she kept her award for Moonstruck. She told him. Unfortunately, a local thief was watching at the time, and afterward he broke into her house and had no problem finding the Academy Award. It was exactly where Olympia said it was. The cat burglar did negotiate with her son for its return, but things never worked out, and her golden guy is still parked on somebody else's mantel.

Don't feel badly for her; she bought a replacement for seventy dollars from the Oscar people. If people argue over paprika, just imagine the husband-wife argument over an Oscar heist:

"Why didn't you turn on the alarm?"
"Why did you have to tell the secret location on TV?"
"Who do you think you are, Ethan Hawke?"
"You mean **Matthew Modine**."
"Never mind."

OH NO, IT'S GERALDO!

When There's an Age Difference

It was the phone call every parent dreads. The child you've raised to maturity has finally decided to marry, and you don't like the person she's picked to spend the rest of her life with.

"On paper this was horrible," Geraldo Rivera told me. "I was four times divorced, a fifty-seven-year-old man, with a notorious reputation, and I wanted to marry their daughter."

That's how television's favorite crusading correspondent remembered the day his girlfriend, twenty-five-year-old Erica Levy, broke the news to her parents, Howard and Nancy, that she was engaged to Geraldo. The phone went dead on the other end.

"They sent their Jewish daughter to meet a nice young Jewish boy," Erica told me. Geraldo was not the boy they had in mind. In fact Geraldo was one year older than her father. Thirty-two years was a big age difference. She was iPod, he was AARP.

The age thing bugged her parents, and that immediately cast a pall over their girl's engagement to the man who went hunting for Bin Laden in the Tora Bora mountains and once caught a chair thrown by a skinhead with his nose.

So Geraldo launched a charm offensive. He invited Erica's parents to fly from their home in Shaker Heights, Ohio, to New York City, where the only network anchor who's widely known by one name would be waiting. He pulled out all the stops in making a terrific first impression.

"I picked them up in my helicopter," Geraldo remembered. (Note to any prospective husbands for my daughters: I don't care how old you are, if you have your own helicopter, you are welcome to marry into my family.) He later shuttled them to Café Des Artistes, a romantic New York landmark where you can dine next to celebrities on forty-seven-dollar Dover sole.

"And we had this talk," Geraldo recalled. He liked her folks. They'd had a rock-solid marriage for more than thirty years. In those same thirty years, Geraldo had been married four times. And his reputation as a ladies' man took off after the publication of his memoir, **Exposing Myself**, which named some very famous people he'd gotten frisky with over the years. (When I read the book, I admired his honesty, but then again, I wasn't marrying him, unless he picked me up in his helicopter.)

Erica's parents listened with laser intensity to the very persuasive and absolutely charming Mr. Rivera. Before this day they'd only known him as the guy with the TV moustache who once did syndicated TV-show segments like "Men in Lace Panties and the Women Who Love Them." That was a long-gone TV persona. In real life, Geraldo is much different. And he let them see who he was. And in an act of "exposing himself" to the visitors from Shaker Heights, he showed them how much he loved their daughter. Geraldo the former attorney had thrown himself upon the mercy of the court and made a persuasive case in his defense, because in the end, the verdict was clear.

"Get married," the parents said.

What was it, he asked, that changed their minds? Geraldo made a personal promise to her father that he would take care of Erica for the rest of her life. Ultimately, isn't that what all parents want for their child?

"At the end of it," Geraldo said, "Erica's dad said to her, 'You're the best.'"

"Now my parents are best of friends with Geraldo," Erica says, beaming. "And his family has opened their arms to me. And I love them so much."

Meanwhile, back in her hometown, the engagement was big news. The Cleveland **Plain Dealer**'s headline barked, CLEVELAND'S OWN CIN-DERELLA STORY, ERICA LEVY. "My parents," Erica said, "called to say, 'Cinderella? It's not like we had you in the basement.'"

They had a fairy-tale wedding, with a party the night before on Geraldo's sailboat, **Voyager,** and a reception at the Four Seasons. The actual ceremony took place at the Central Synagogue in New York, so at least his in-laws got their wish for a Jewish wedding. Geraldo wanted to make a statement to his boldfaced friends in attendance. "I really wanted to announce to people, whatever your misgivings or desire to make light or fun of (our marriage), just look at us!"

Plenty looked. In attendance were Bill and Hillary Clinton, some other world leaders, gossip-page regulars, and paratroopers from the 101st and 82nd Airborne. And while other couples work hard to make sure that somebody doesn't cause a scene, Geraldo threw caution to the wind and invited Israel's former prime minster **and** the Palestinians' chief negotiator. No fists flew; champagne did. And so did the jabs about the bride and groom's vast age disparity.

Geraldo's best man, the actor Cheech Marin, made a toast that started as a shot at Erica but wound up taking out her new husband. "Once she finally gets cranky at forty," Marin said, looking at Geraldo, "you'll be dead."

Later Erica's father, Howard, let the one-year-older Geraldo have it. He recounted a father-and-future-son-in-law bonding experience, when they traveled to the Rock and Roll Hall of Fame in Cleveland. "When we went to purchase the tickets, the ticket-booth guy says, 'Two senior citizens tickets, fellas?'"

So there it was, the elephant in the middle of the room. This husband and wife are not the same age. They are three decades and two years apart. It's no big deal to them, so why should it be to anybody else?

"With Geraldo it's not really an issue, he's so young," his wife said, beaming. "He's so energetic. It's hard for me to keep up with him, because he's in great shape."

"She's really my social guide for the cultural realities of life," Geraldo explained. "She's my bridge to the modern era."

Erica helps her husband relate to a different generation. He does the same for her. "I think that I'm an Elvis and Bob Dylan and Vietnam person," Geraldo told me. "Those were the formative years for me. And she's in a much different era."

"I listen to the same music," Erica says. "Bob Dylan is now **my** favorite."

"We've been together five years, and we scarcely argue," Geraldo added as I realized the generation gap I'd imagined from the outside didn't exist inside their marriage.

"She has my back," said Mr. Rivera. "And I know that is where my comfort is. I come home to my baby, I come home to my wife's arms. It's a nest where, whatever the perils of the universe, they can't assail me."

"I feel very lucky," the bride said, blushing.

Her husband concluded, "I've finally figured out, this is the hand I want to play until the end of the game."

Let's face it, age is just a number. I know some sixty-year-olds who have the bodies of people in their forties, just as I know some thirty-somethings who act as if they're seventy-five and just waiting for a shuffleboard court to open up in Fort Lauderdale.

Here's the key: Always remember that in our **hearts**, we're all the same age.

How to Make the "Just Married" Feeling Last Forever
(According to an Old Joke)

How to impress a woman: Wine her, dine her, smile at her, laugh with her, cuddle her, do whatever she wants.

How to impress a man: Show up naked, with beer.

RULES OF ENGAGEMENT

Married in the Military

Army guys I know who had to find temporary lodging in New York City would often ask to be housed at a particular executive hotel on the East Side of Manhattan. Why there? It wasn't because it was in the heart of the city, or it had easy access in and out of town. The reason men in uniform forcefully asked for this place was that the number one occupation of the people who permanently lived there was flight attendant.

A famous TV general told me, "Guys would find out about this place and say, 'If I have to be in New York, I want to live in **that** place.'"

This, ladies and gentlemen, is why we have the finest fighting force on the face of the planet. Our warriors are brilliant when it comes to finding chicks.

A colonel and his three buddies from the Presidio in San Francisco were temporarily assigned to New York for a short course on Wall Street, and knowing the building's reputation, they immediately drew up a battle plan.

"We wanted to have a Sunday brunch and meet some women. So we put up flyers in the lobby and the elevator. Sixteen girls showed up."

The colonel met a very attractive model that day. She was not impressed with his homemaking skills.

"When I walked into that apartment, he was in the kitchen," she remembered. "He had eighty-five pieces of bacon hanging over the skillet, and a two-cup percolator."

A week or two later the army guys put up another flyer in the elevator inviting the entire building to a champagne brunch (man does not live by MRE alone).

"They turned out in droves," the colonel told me with a grin.

Once again the model and the cute colonel crossed paths. They chatted a bit more. After a few martinis, he asked her out to dinner. "Because I knew that the way to get a woman's heart in New York was to invite her out to eat."

"I was too poor to spend that kind of money," she said. "He said to me, 'Where are you from?' And I said, 'Kind of everywhere. My father's in the army.'

"'Oh my God,' he groaned. 'I went three thousand miles to meet an army brat!'"

It was probably the influence of her father, but she did love men in uniform. She wasn't exclusively army.

Would she go out with a marine? "In a heartbeat."

How about a sailor? "Absolutely. I'm easy."

Coast Guard? "Sure," she said. "Merchant marine would be hard, because they're gone so much." Scratch them off the list.

Actually, she suddenly had only one guy on her list, the bacon-eating, champagne-brunch-catering colonel.

"She was out fishing when I met her," he said, "and she caught me."

They'd met in March. By June she was his date for his West Point reunion, and the next weekend he proposed. Her mother took the next plane to meet the future groom. Her father (then a colonel too) didn't meet her intended until four days before the wedding.

"Thank God he's got short hair," the mother reported to her co-commanding officer on a secure phone line.

"It's not easy being married to somebody in the military. There's always the worry that something will go wrong," she told me. Her mother had been a bride of just two weeks when Pearl Harbor was attacked. Her father, coincidentally, was stationed at the Presidio, and after the attack he went to work one day and simply disappeared.

"My mom knew he was part of D-day but didn't know where he'd ended up or even if he was alive. As long as that horrible military vehicle didn't drive up to the front of the house, there was hope."

Six weeks after Omaha Beach, her mother got a letter. "I'm all right," he assured her. She could start breathing again. For six weeks she hadn't known if her husband was dead or alive, and there were thousands of other American wives in exactly the same boat. That's just the way things worked back then, before e-mail and satellite phone.

As of this writing our couple that met at the stewardess hotel in New York has been married more than thirty years. He proudly served his country, and she proudly followed him from base to base with their family in tow. When married men or women serve in the military, their spouses discover that while they might not wear a uniform, they also sacrifice a lot. I salute them. It's not easy, and they don't get much encouragement.

"There were so many wives I'd meet who'd never experienced army life," she said. "They didn't know rank" and what it meant that their husband's boss was a captain and the significance of the Stars and Stripes. "They didn't understand why their husbands would have to go away for so long, and the hardships they'd have to endure.

The young wives would come to me because they didn't understand why I seemed so much stronger.

"I would use my mother as my role model, because I watched her as she went through it all, starting with World War II. I think one of the things that made it easier was that I was an army brat."

It takes a special person to selflessly serve his or her country, and it takes another special person to be married to that person. It is a hard life. What's the key? I asked my camouflaged husband-and-wife team, who are now retired and live the good life at their bunker resort in Montana.

"Number one is communication," she told me. "And that's followed by sense of humor. They go hand in hand. If you don't have that in a marriage, it's not going to be strong."

But what happens when after years of living apart you're suddenly together under the same roof day after day? When they start to bug each other, what do they do?

"I go work out, or take the dog for a run," he nonchalantly answered in the tone of a man who'd just gone for a run, with the dog.

She had a better idea. Her solution combined her desire to get him out of the house with a skill he'd developed at the expense of the Pentagon. "I'll tell him, 'Why don't you go outside and shoot something?'"

And he does.

GIMME SHELTER

Your First Home

I have lived in fourteen different houses. That total does not include the luxurious double-wide I briefly called home while attending the University of Kansas. You know the calculus on that: Kansas + mobile home + tornadoes = Last place to live in twister season.

I have always tried to make my bachelor pads as comfortable as possible without going over to the dark side of interior design, where things match. That all changed when I married my wife, who felt that the eight-person Jacuzzi in the living room just didn't say "family man." It was time to move to the suburbs.

We had the same checklist everybody has. A house with a white picket fence, a yard to mow, a dog to feed, and a tiny mortgage. The American Dream.

It does not exist.

Welcome to the world of real estate. Or real misstate. The jargon takes some getting used to.

- "Fixer-uppers" should be called "starter-overs."
- "Quaint" translates to "was stylish when Eisenhower was president."

- "Low taxes" means resources are scarce and the closest public school to your quaint, fix-er-upper has only one book in its library.

The best way to find a new house is to drive around and find a neighborhood you like. Don't move into areas that are scary or apt to flood, or into a house whose last owner was the EPA Superfund.

We were driving through Virginia and saw a lovely neighborhood with rolling hills and grazing horses inside white board fences. "Honey, they have fences," my wife said. It reminded me of my childhood in the joint.

We found a place we liked; in fact, it seemed too good to be true. There had to be a catch. Maybe there had been a horrible murder there and the walls bled when there's a full moon. Who cared? It had a 45,000-gallon swimming pool! My wife gave me that "This house would make me happy" look, and I started a fifteen-second negotiation with the real estate agent.

"This is what we're looking for," I gushed. "It's perfect!" And in a statement they're still using at Harvard Business School to demonstrate how not to negotiate, I went on: "Whatever the owners are asking, that'll probably be fine with us."

I should also point out that we bought the house after seeing only the living room and the swimming pool. It's a good thing there were bed-rooms upstairs, or we would have had to install bunk beds in the front hall. We were impulse shoppers, who'd had a couple of drinks with dinner.

Over the years in that house we realized we'd probably paid too much and that next time, we'd do it differently. Fast-forward seven years, and I was being lured back to New York for a television job. The last time I'd been in New York we'd had just one kid and a six-thousand-dollar-a-month one-bedroom rental. (NBC paid, back before they sank all their money into **Fear Factor 9**.) Why was the unit so expensive? An East River view, and Garbo was our next-door neighbor. At least that's what the Realtor told us. In reality the only time we saw the famous recluse was the day the coroner toe-tagged her and carted her out.

Now we had three children, and I discovered most families of five don't live in New York City, where double strollers are as rare as a Wal-Mart on Park Avenue. People wind up living in the so-called Tristate area—New Jersey, Connecticut, or New York. After three months, and nine real estate agents (including one who said, "I've seen your show; maybe you should consider renting"), we bought a house in New Jersey, the Garden Apartment State.

The house had everything we needed: a roof, walls, paint. But more important, it was available exactly when our other house sale was closing. So we bought it, without ever actually going **inside** the house first. I know you're thinking, "How do these nitwits put their pants on in the morning?" Just like you, one leg at a time, over our heads. There's a logical explanation. The owners and their children had the measles, mumps, or bird flu, and we thought, "Why chance disease?" We paid their asking price.

On moving day, we were delighted to discover that our new home was well built and beautifully decorated in a never-before-seen hue of pink. Palace O' Pepto-Bismol. We weren't crazy about that color scheme, so we eventually replaced it with Matte Maalox.

A MOVING EXPERIENCE

Relocating Your Family

Sixty-seven hundred cans of Orange Crush soda were between our new house and us.

Why that semi jackknifed and spilled its load across six lanes of traffic, we didn't know. But the delay gave us plenty of time to reflect on our new home and new life. It's never a good idea to have idle time on your hands after you've just signed a thirty-year mortgage that obligates you to pay for what I now worried was an overpriced, poorly drained hellhole.

It started out as a traffic accident, but upon forensic review, it appeared it may also have been an omen. "Stop now, turn around, and go back!"

the Ouija board would have screamed, if we'd had the travel version.

Two hours later we'd crossed the Orange Sea and were curbside at our new home. We would move in as soon as the previous owners moved out. They were running late. They had a pickup, a box truck, and two U-Hauls on my just-purchased lawn as an army of beefy men ran in and out of the house dragging boxes and appliances. It looked less like moving day and more like an evacuation. The only thing missing was a helicopter landing on the roof to extract the family.

"Give us an hour," the former owner said. So we went out to eat. When we returned they were gone, and we discovered why they were making a speedy retreat. Apparently as soon as we had agreed to buy the place six weeks earlier, the owners suspended the intensive housecleaning that Realtors insist upon. On the stove gleamed a lovely patina of shimmering grease, and in the toilets a creepy black fungus was flourishing. What kind of antioxidant-free diet were they on?

"Hey, that's not a Gummi Bear!" I yelled at my daughter, who'd been crawling on the floor and had located something she was at that moment jamming into her mouth. It certainly wasn't a cookie. It was a fifty-cent-piece-sized bit of decorative glass. The fact that it was decorative did not make me feel any better.

The owners were obligated to leave the house "broom clean," and they probably did, but my wife was hysterical. "Who do I call at the CDC to quarantine this block?" Our real estate agent saw a storm brewing and called a cleaning company. The crew chief arrived within an hour. I presumed he was there to start cleaning. No, he was there simply to make an estimate. After the guy walked through the house with a clipboard and tape measure, he presented his report. The job would take a crew of eight men twelve hours to clean, at a cost of $2,700. After I checked the room for a **Candid Camera** crew, I realized he was serious. I told him I couldn't afford that—I worked in cable.

"How much to clean just the kitchen and bath-rooms?" I inquired. He went back to his supercom-puter and came up with a more affordable $1,300.

My wife, another hard bargainer, said, "Fine, whatever it takes. I'm not sleeping in this filthy house." The reason I agreed was the former own-ers had already given us $1,200 in case anything was broken. I'd hoped to pocket that cash, but instead it would go to a good cause—to de-Crisco-ize the stove and to kill that creature that just tried to drag one of the kids underneath it.

So they started the $1,200 project; in the end they did a better job cleaning out my wallet than cleaning the house. Then the movers, who'd been waiting patiently with their friend Sam Adams, came in with our life's possessions. As they pulled out, the driver, who'd sucked down six or seven beers, backed the eighteen-wheeler directly across my new neighbor's yard. I'm not talking grazing the edge of the grass; it went smack-dab across the center. And thanks to a half an inch of rain earlier in the day that left the ground soft and mushy, there were now four sets of two-inch-deep tire tracks across the middle of their lawn.

"Go over and apologize to your neighbor right now," our horrified real estate agent instructed. What was I supposed to say? "Ad-lib something, or else they'll hate you every day of your life in this house." As I perp-walked over, I noticed it wasn't just grass, it was freshly laid sod. And they had a new Lexus parked in the driveway. "Uh-oh," I thought to myself, "they're loaded. I bet they're lawyers…"

Knock knock knock. Nothing. Another couple of knocks. Nobody answered. I returned to my new home where my real estate agent had an interesting take on the situation. "You know, if they're not home, that means they didn't see it happen. They can't pin it on you!" Right. It was just a **coincidence** that the day we moved in, a renegade 767 pilot did some practice landings on their front lawn. The agent left, and we celebrated our new home with a trip to the emergency room for a round of tetanus shots.

The next day, I was back at the neighbor's door. **Knock knock knock.**

No life-forms moving in the house. I had to do something to fix the lawn, so I went to my garage and found a rake. For the next thirty minutes, I tried to groom the grass. Because I didn't know what my neighbors looked like, every time a car would approach, I'd run back and start raking my lawn, which thanks to the previous owner's U-Haul evacuation was also wagon-wheeled.

Operation Fescue Rescue continued for the next three days. In the morning I'd knock on the door, nobody would answer, and then I'd try again to camouflage the mess. My landscape work didn't help much. It still looked like somebody had staged a NASCAR event in their front yard.

On day four, around eight in the evening, we spotted some headlights in the neighbor's driveway. Finally, they were home. At sunup it would be time to face the music. At 8:05, our doorbell rang. I opened the door. It was a police officer. With a gun. Thank goodness it was holstered, so I could make a run for it before he started to pistol-whip me. Just then two of my preschool-aged children, who'd just concluded their first bath in their newly sanitized tub, barreled down the stairs to greet our first guest. Did I mention they were nude and only marginally dry?

"Good evening, sir," he said, staring at the naked toddlers. "Do you know your neighbors in the gray house?"

"No, we just moved in a couple of days ago," I answered in that innocent voice the clearly guilty always use on crime shows. "Officer, it was our moving truck that did all that damage."

"Damage?" He cocked his head to hear better.

Uh-oh. Was he testing me? Playing dumb to get me to admit what happened? I looked down and could see my own face reflected in his chrome badge. It was like I had been given sodium Pentothal. I started singing like a canary. "Damage to their lawn. Our movers grazed their lawn a little bit." I stretched the truth in the same way you'd describe a cat-five hurricane as doing "a little roof damage."

"All right, I'll make a notation of that," he said. A notation. That didn't sound so bad. **Notation** was better than **citation.** That's when he lowered the boom.

"I'm not here about the lawn. Your neighbors are missing, and I was here to see if you might know their whereabouts."

Terrific. I'd just admitted to a cop that I'd destroyed their personal property and now had a clear motive for making my wealthy neighbors disappear. They'd start dredging the local rivers in the morning. The jig was up.

THE MR. & MRS. HAPPY HANDBOOK | 107

"Their nephew is looking for them, so I'm going to leave a note. If you talk to them, tell them to call me." The cop shoved his business card my way.

A card? A note? Where was the crime-scene tape, the dusting for prints, the Bad Cop to go with the Good Cop?

"Thanks for your help," he said, and he left.

"That was weird" was my first reaction. What kind of a place is this neighborhood, where people disappear for the better part of a week and don't tell blood relatives where they've gone?

The next morning a silver Honda was in the driveway next to the previously abandoned Lexus. An elegant woman in a housecoat and slippers greeted me after I **knock knock knocked**.

"Hello," she said.

"Hi, I'm your new neighbor—" I started.

"Welcome," she interrupted.

"Thanks. Listen, when we moved in, our truck ran over your front yard," I said, pointing behind me to the two-inch-deep ruts. "I'm really, really sorry."

"Don't worry about the lawn, we have a service," she said.

What? A service would come to her house and iron out the kinks in her front lawn? Great. Maybe when they were done they could iron out the wrinkles in my forehead.

"All right, then," I said, so relieved that she wasn't mad. "I'm glad I stopped by. One more thing. Call the police—they think you're dead."

MR. HAPPY'S ADVICE

Moving day is when buyer's remorse hits you. Why did we move here? Why did we spend so much? Why didn't we notice that leaking dioxin plant in the backyard?

Over time, most people who stay in their new homes realize that the move was worth it. And all those humongous problems on day one weren't that gigantic after all.

So what if our house was a little untidy? You should see it now. The key is flexibility. "Adjust on the fly, or you're going to cry."

Wherever you move, remember it's your Home Sweet Home, the best place on earth, if you don't count that duplex that is currently available next to the Dallas Cowboy Cheerleader Training Camp.

THE ALIENS NEXT DOOR

Your Neighbors

If you do an inventory of my garage right now, you'll find that I have my neighbor's retractable ladder, hedge trimmer, and chain saw (which will not be returned until they buy it a new chain so I can finally cut down that limb over my chimney). Meanwhile, I'm still waiting for various neighbors to return a DustBuster, a Rabbit corkscrew, and my son's Curious George lunch box.

Neighbors are good for one thing: whatever you need right now.

Why go to the store, when you know that chances are if you need a cup of sugar, a pint of Guinness, or three ounces of Kryptonite, there is somebody on your block who probably has it? All you've got to do is ask. That's good. But most neighborhoods are on two-way streets, and that means at the most critical part of the big game your doorbell will ring and your neighbor from four doors down will first ask how everything's been going over the last nine months, follow that up with more aimless small talk, then finally get around to asking you the question that brought him to your door. "Do you have anything to patch the liner of my Esther Williams aboveground pool?"

"Actually I do, but it's going to take a minute to find." You'll disappear to the basement and return with a tiny tube of stuff you'll hand to the thankful neighbor and arrive back at your chair just as the ESPN announcer reminds the audience that they've just witnessed the biggest comeback in the history of sports.

I love most of my neighbors. Some bug me, big-time. Chances are you've got good neighbors and bad neighbors as well. If NASA is looking for a volunteer family for a twenty-year mission to Jupiter, I'd like to sign some of my neighbors up.

Here's why. Their dog constantly runs into our yard and bites our dog, which thanks to an invisible fence is trapped at home, just waiting for another yard invasion. Their mutt has actually clawed its way into our home, through a screen door, only to trap my wife in the laundry room, then poop on the antique rug that was my grandmother's.

I also blame them for their kids, who'll ring the doorbell at 7 A.M. Saturday to ask if they can come in and play with my kids. Of course they can't, because my kids are sleeping. So then they'll camp out on my front porch until nine, when they'll ring again and wake up the house for the day. That's when one of my kids will invite them in.

Raising my own kids was hard enough, but raising my neighbors' as well is something I don't want to do, unless I get some sort of a tax break. Usually after we feed them lunch, I'll say, "I think it's time you should go home."

"Oh, I can't, my parents take naps about now," the neighbor kid says, as he removes another box of Ritz Bits from our pantry. "Mommy said we should stay all day." Pinch me, I'm dreaming. The people down the street whose dog regularly terrorizes us are now deploying their children to our home, for brunches and lunches, because THEY'RE ASLEEP?

Eventually they leave, but finally I put down my foot and instructed my wife and kids that "under no circumstances" were they to allow those neighbor kids into the house ever again.

"Daddy," my littlest inquired, "could we let them in if space aliens destroyed their home?"

"Sure, honey, but **only** if it's first declared a total loss by State Farm Insurance. So ask to speak to an adjuster."

So imagine my surprise two days later when I arrived home after a grueling day at the office to discover the neighbor kids, with their babysitter, in my house. Inexplicably, the babysitter was holding a live chicken.

She didn't speak much English, and when I asked why she had brought the bird into our home, she simply said, **"Sí."**

The time line of what happened next is uncertain, but we do know that it was about the time one of the neighbor kids pulled a butterfly out of his pocket to show my daughter how it could fly **in**

the house that the chicken, apparently spooked, broke loose from the babysitter.

Luckily, the chicken did not fly. But it did run around and scare the living daylights out of my children, who are more comfortable with a chicken that has been dipped in bread crumbs and fried golden brown. A bug-eyed, clucking, pecking machine could terrorize a kid of any age, and that's what we had.

Fortunately, our dog was there to chase the bird from the kitchen to the dining room, where he caught it. Then he brought it back into the great room, where he did his best to send it to that big coop in the sky.

There's something about a golden retriever— once it's got food in its vicinity, there's nothing short of an improvised explosive device that will get that food source out of its jaws. Nothing. I tried and wound up with a two-inch gash on my hand that used up our entire supply of Star Wars Band-Aids.

So as that monarch butterfly fluttered above the crime scene, our dog finished up his chicken dinner fit for the Colonel. We could do nothing but watch and wait. And once the meal was finished, about the only thing left of the bird was that red wattle thing that hangs from the beak. The babysitter picked up the remains and headed to the door.

We had stood there in slack-jawed silence as it occurred, and I knew this was my last chance to make my point. "It would probably be a good thing if you don't bring any more chickens into our house."

"Sí."

MRS. HAPPY'S ADVICE

Most neighbors are terrific. When there is illness or a death in your family, they show up with a lasagna and salad. They drive your kids to school when you're stuck. They go to their pantries when you ask them if they can spare a quart of olive oil, a single beef bouillon cube, or a pair of handcuffs.

But they are easy to hate when things go wrong. Your neighbor is not always a person; sometimes he is that barking dog, that loose chicken, that pile of leaves accidentally dumped on your side of the lawn.

So if your neighbors bug you, here's what you do. Nothing. Don't yell at them. Don't gossip about them. Don't scheme how to smoke them out with an "accidental garage fire" that the authorities could easily trace back to you.

Remember, if you do them wrong, they'll stab you in the back the first chance they get. Your neighbors are the first ones the cops will interview when you're missing.

"Oh, they're gone? Did you check downstairs in his crystal-meth lab?"

"Crystal meth?"

"Yes," they'll report. "I hear it tastes like chicken."

MR. HANDY

Home Remodeling

One morning while I was making my daily appearance on **Fox & Friends,** I spotted this incoming e-mail among assorted blogs and hate mail.

"Dad, call home—there's water pouring out of the kitchen lights."

The fact that it was authored by the very tall boy who lived at my house was alarming enough, but as a longtime Bob Vila viewer I know that water isn't supposed to pour out of kitchen lights.

During the next commercial I phoned home and discovered that the waterfall began shortly after my wife started a load of laundry. So I told her to turn off the washer, and like magic, the water stopped pouring out of the lights. Crisis averted, the kids returned to their Cap'n Crunch.

When I got home I realized I'd forgotten to put the washer hose back in the drain the day before when I'd finished remodeling the laundry room. When the washer hit its drain cycle, it drained onto the floor, down the wall, through the lights.

Just another day in the life of a do-it-your-selfer (DIYer). I come from a long line of handy guys. My father would cut off his own arm with a butter knife before he'd hire a professional to do something around the house. That means I grew up with an unpainted living room, kitchen cabinets with no doors, and gray gravel where the driveway was supposed to be.

I believe there are two Americas. No, not red states and blue states, but DIYers and Hire-a-Guy-ers.

Most people I know hire guys to mow their lawns, paint their houses, fix their faucets, and do the things that husbands once did. You can easily spot Hire-a-Guy families; they're the ones having fun. Meanwhile, the DIYers are at Home Depot, listening to a guy in an orange apron explain the correct way to light the water-heater pilot so you don't blow up your house.

Most young married couples are on a budget and wind up becoming DIYers. That's why my wife early in our marriage brought home nine rolls of painfully overpriced wallpaper. She reasoned we could afford it because she'd put it up herself. She was new to the wallpaper game and didn't quite understand seams and directions. When I arrived home she asked me to survey her work. It was really something. She'd glued the paper to the wall perfectly backward. We had 180 square feet of upside-down flower arrangements. It looked like Satan's garden.

Aside from incorrect installation, there's always the danger of bodily harm. When I was remodeling one kitchen in Virginia (the Who Needs a Permit State), I discovered the hard way that fiberglass insulation, which looks like pink cotton candy, "is actually glass." The doctor at the emergency room told me this as he fished it out of the eye with the newly ripped cornea.

"I told you to hire somebody," my loving wife reminded me as she drove me home with my left eye patched and bandaged. "Did you hear me, Popeye?" Popeye nodded.

Another time I'd been chatting with my wife on the deck when I decided I was going to paint the deck right that minute. I started removing the kids' toys. "Relax," she said. "Do it over the weekend."

But as is the case with most DIYers, I was a bullhead. "Must paint deck now, must paint deck now."

So I fished the deck stain out of the basement, found my long-nap roller covers, and asked my son to stir the stain as I cleared off the deck. I was carrying a Little Tikes Cozy Coupe down the **Architectural Digest**–worthy staircase that I'd built the summer before when a shooting pain went through the back of my leg. It felt just like an ice pick. That resulted in my unfortunate decision to take the final nine steps in one giant leap. I crashed on top of the car. (Note to Ralph Nader: The Cozy Coupe air bag did not deploy; please investigate.)

My five-year-old son ran to my side and asked if I needed the Booboo Bear (an icy toy that magically makes tears stop whenever it flash-freezes a body part). "Get Mommy," I groaned.

"Should I call the ambulance?"

"Get Mommy," I croaked, and he disappeared. In moments of great pain, DIYers are also amateur physicians, so I looked at the back of my leg to diagnose the problem. I was expecting to see that I'd been impaled by something. Instead there were just two puncture holes, three quarters of an inch apart. I didn't need an EMT for a second opinion; I'd been snake-bitten! With the snake venom circulating through my bloodstream, I wondered where my wife was. Somebody needed to suck the poison out of my leg before it got to my heart and sent me to that big workshop in the sky.

She was nowhere to be seen, but my three-year-old daughter was coming down the stairs yelling, "I come help, I come help Daddy," when she hit the same step on which I had gotten bitten and let out a bloodcurdling scream. **"Aaaarrrrrrrgggrragaghhhhh!"** Oh, the humanity! Another family member taken out! But unlike me, she didn't fall into a doughy ball; she stood there and took it like a man. Hearing **her** scream, my wife bolted out of the house.

Attending first to the nonbreadwinner, my wife announced that she had just one puncture hole. Clearly that meant a snake fang had broken in my leg. She loves me, but I knew she would never suck out the venom if there was a tooth in there. It wouldn't be long now…Steve…walk toward the light…

She looked at my leg, said not a word, and then taking her life in her hands, walked over to the husband-built staircase and peered underneath where the anaconda had tried to take out her next of kin.

"There's a hornet's nest," she announced.

Okay, so maybe there wasn't a snake fang in my leg, but there was a stinger, which was the only thing I could feel. My body sent my foot into shock to hide the fact that I had four broken bones in it and had ripped most of the ligaments off the bone.

I went to the emergency room, where the physician who'd pulled the insulation out of my eye set my cast.

The next day, on crutches and Demerol, I painted the deck.

Look, DIYers are not trained craftsmen. We look at household problems and try to solve them with logic. But eventually we come to a project for which there is no how-to book and we have to figure it out ourselves. That, I have found, is always a deeply satisfying feeling when you can analyze a problem and formulate a plan of attack. Plus, you know you're saving a ton of money by not calling in a professional.

One morning at about three-thirty, I was backing out of my garage en route to work when I realized I'd made the unfortunate mistake of neglecting to open the garage door first. The crash woke up the entire house. My wife said, "I thought **Sputnik** hit the roof!" But that noise was tiny compared to the sound later in the day when I tried to fix the dented garage door myself. I'd assessed the problem. Bent door, pulley and springs in wrong location.

"Don't do it" was the last thing my wife said to me as I went outside to loosen a bolt. The four-hundred-pound door collapsed on top of my newly leased car.

Now I'm officially a Hire-a-Guy.

The car-insurance adjuster did not buy the hailstorm story.

MR. HAPPY'S ADVICE

A Harris Interactive survey says that 72 percent of women say their ideal man spends his free time doing home improvement projects. You may be that man.

Congratulations. I'm that man and I'm driving my wife nuts.

My advice is, go ahead and try the easy stuff. You can paint things, replace lightbulbs, and mow your own lawn. I think.

However, when it comes to tricky stuff like electricity, plumbing, major construction, or dented doors, call somebody who needs to make a Lexus payment.

KING OF PAIN

Should I Go to the Hospital?

Why this was hushed up in the mainstream media, I have no idea, but Richard Simmons, the bedazzled exercise guru who taught the world how to "sweat to the oldies," broke my nose.

It happened during a commercial break (no pun intended) early one morning on **Fox & Friends**. With only a few seconds left before we went live again, the stage manager threw me a prop box to hold on the air. Richard Simmons, whose catlike reflexes kicked in, saw the box heading in what he thought was his direction and redirected it straight toward my nose.

As we returned from the commercial, everybody was laughing about it, but it was no joke in the emergency room. The admitting nurse, followed by the orderly and then the X-ray technician, all individually asked variations of this question: "The guy in the extra-short shorts broke your nose?" Go ahead, laugh away at my bulbous blower.

Once upon a time my lap-sized son asked if he could hitch a ride on the lawn mower with me, despite my wife saying, "Over my dead body!" She was not dead, but she was off-site, and I rationalized she'd never know what the men did with the power tools while she was absent.

The grin on my son's face was wall to wall as he sat squarely on my lap helping me mow. This was what being a dad was all about, spending quality time with my sole male heir engaged in this quasi-dangerous activity. We were on the last lap when disaster struck.

Upon review, I probably should have known better than to attempt to mow the really steep hill out by the street. Suddenly my eighteen-horsepower mower from Sears (Where America Shops for Dangerous Stuff) was tipping over on its side.

"Daddy, we're flying!" my son gleefully screamed, thinking that I'd planned mowing on two wheels.

"Hold on!" I said in that quaky "Dad's in trouble" voice. My first priority was to keep him on my lap, so I balanced him **away** from the ground. However, that meant I was nudging him in the general direction of the now exposed spinning mower blades that are supposed to cut grass but that were, at that moment, closer to cutting hair. As I jammed my foot to the ground, to prevent a complete rollover, my leg got caught in the sheet metal, ripping a huge gash in my once cute thigh. I also turned in the direction we were tipping, and the crisis was averted.

During the near-rollover, I'd leaned us both forward to stay in the seat, and I'd knocked my son's nose into the steering wheel. He burst into tears, just as my wife pulled into the driveway. She was not happy. I'd already donated half a unit of blood to my lawn, but my wife, who was running from the car, didn't even notice me.

"We were flying, Mommy!" I heard him say as she drove off with him to the emergency room. Once there, my wife discovered that a crying boy with a bloody nose is sometimes the victim of child abuse, so once the bleeding stopped she was escorted out and the doctor turned into Sergeant Joe Friday.

This instantly horrified my wife. Our little angel could say a million things, nothing illegal— in this country—but you never know what a kid will say. He had always been very verbal and had no trouble telling the attending physician exactly what happened. "My dad was mowing and we started flying and then I hit my schnozz."

Thank goodness we were in the clear. He told the truth and didn't add anything extra, like the time his father jammed an inch-long sliver under a fingernail and said some words that he'd never heard on Shining Time Station. But his parents did notice one thing, he'd said "schnozz" to describe his nose. "Schnozz?" Who was writing his lines, Jackie Mason?

An hour later, when it was my turn to go in for stitches and my twice-yearly tetanus shot, the doctor told me why he had to ask those questions and what my son had said.

I thanked him for his concern, and then I gave him some friendly advice. I told him that if I were a doctor examining somebody with a bloody nose, the first thing I'd ask would be Richard Simmons's whereabouts.

MR. HAPPY'S ADVICE

Never carpool on a John Deere product that has a beer caddy.

If you ever question whether an injury is worthy of a trip to the doctor, just go. Better safe than sorry. Always seek treatment if there is blood, a bone, or a lawsuit visible.

WHEN I'M DEAD, SHE'S RICH

Wife Insurance

When I started working in Washington, D.C., I thought I had plenty of life insurance, and for a single guy I did. How much would it cost to feed in perpetuity my pet, G. Gordon Kitty? Then I got hitched, and it wouldn't be long before my cat was banished to Hair Ball Hell.

A year after we'd gotten married my wife, who was at the time six months pregnant, had numerous new "financial" hormones floating around in her bloodstream. That's the only explanation I can come up with for why she shook me awake in the middle of the night. At first I thought there was an intruder downstairs. Nope. She'd had an epiphany.

"You need more life insurance. We need protection."

Protection? She should have thought about that six months earlier, when there was a clear and present danger that my sketchy cat would sneak into my room to suck the air out of my lungs. The next day I started my quest for quotes.

Educated consumers always get the best rates and plans, so I researched which insurance company to call, based upon the company with the best TV commercial. Companies had ads that were either funny or tearjerkers. I figured if they were laughing in the commercial, they'd be howling when my heirs called for a payout. So the serious company got my business.

The insurance agent arrived at our modest starter home at the appointed time. Just like his company's commercial, he was very professional, all business. Sure, he tried to get me to fall for that "universal life" policy that would have built a new wing on his home, but I needed my money more than he needed a winter vacation in Zermatt, so I opted for the term policy, which in plain language guaranteed my heirs cash when I'm term-inated.

Once we settled on a plan, I had to apply for the policy. They would look at my information and see if I was a good risk—in other words, if I was about to drop dead for some reason, in which case they didn't want my business. They were looking for customers whose heart rate and cholesterol levels were in the single digits. To enable them to assess their risk, I had to submit to an intimate line of questioning. Mr. Insurance asked me about any physical problems, past drug use, sexual weirdness, and even if I had a tattoo. I felt like I was on **The Maury Povich Show.** "Yes, I'm the baby's daddy!" as the crowd applauds.

After the third degree, I felt like I needed a fifth, because he then asked me to roll up my sleeve and give two vials of blood. That scared me. First of all, I was using all my blood, right that minute, and second, he was **an insurance guy with a syringe.** "Why?" I asked.

He explained that if I wanted a lot of coverage, the insurance company wanted to make sure I was a suitable risk and wasn't hooked on drugs or afflicted by lousy lipid levels, and (and we're back to the Maury show) that I didn't have a sexually transmitted disease.

Those were all things I wanted answers to anyway, so I rolled up a sleeve and he tapped out a vein. Three days later the report would come back: "You're approved," which is insurance code for "You don't have gonorrhea."

The questioning, the blood donation—it all had me on edge, but it turned my wife into quite the kidder. After my exam, he asked how much coverage we needed. "How much would you suggest?" I inquired. He suggested that we buy enough so he could make a Jaguar payment.

"I don't know the exact amount," my wife started in that grieving-widow voice, "but I'm going to need a lot when my husband passes on."

She didn't say "if" her husband passes on, she said "when." For a moment I considered checking the Yellow Pages for a professional food tester. The agent swiveled around to look the eager widow in the eye.

She continued, "Of course we need to provide for the baby."

The agent was nodding like one of those dogs in the back windows of a car.

"And then I'll have needs…I'll need a new wardrobe. I've been out of circulation for a while, and I'll need to replace everything I've got." He stopped nodding and started sweating. "Widows can't wear black forever," she told him.

Then he asked whether the clothes would be for job interviewing or working, a thought she immediately tamped down.

"Oh no. My husband wouldn't want me to work. I'll need the new wardrobe because I'll be dating around, a lot." That's when she actually winked at him. His pocket protector went limp.

Despite already being dead and having my widow buying up whole racks of ready-to-wear at Neiman Marcus, I thought I should say something because the agent looked scared. "Sir, she's just kidding."

"No I'm not!" she barked. Then shifting back into her smoky cocktail voice, she said, "You know"—here she leaned toward the agent—"I'd have an affair, if I could just get a sitter!"

That's when he made the same kind of fur-ball coughing noise my former cat would make. "I believe I've got everything I need," he said as he gathered the papers, had me sign in three places, and ran out of our house like he was being chased by a rabid Old Yeller.

The policy arrived two weeks later.

She's still waiting to collect and date.

MR. HAPPY'S ADVICE

Get as much coverage as you can afford. Just know that your family may actually live higher on the hog when you're gone.

I've taken care of my children's educational needs and a stipend for my wife to live out her days in modest comfort. However, the only way she'll really be loaded when I check out is if they strike oil when they dig the hole.

PET OF THE YEAR

Animal House

So you're thinking about getting a pet. Before you go to that store at the mall with the yapping cocker spaniels in the window, just know that as of today, our dog has cost us $327,090. I'm not kidding.

Whenever the L. L. Bean catalog would arrive with a cover featuring a yellow Labrador flushing out a pheasant or when we'd surf over to the TV Land channel and see Timmy falling down a mine shaft, only to be saved by Lassie, our kids would say, "Can we get a dog? Please?"

They'd begged for thirteen years. Finally they wore us down until we felt like brake pads on a 1972 Pinto. Christmas morning a note arrived, in Santa's handwriting, with the good news: our family would get a dog that year. There were cheers, there were tears, and then forty-five seconds later they resumed watching **The E! True Hollywood Story: Anna Nicole Smith.**

They spent six months researching "the good" (collie), "the bad" (Doberman), and "the ugly" (shar-pei), and came to the conclusion that they wanted a dog that looked like it belonged in the family. Since we're all blond, we went with the golden retriever, the Breck Girl of the dog world.

We located a breeder in Princeton, New Jersey, and bought a sixteen-hundred-dollar purebred, direct descendant of a dog that once won something at the Westminster Dog Show, we think. After all those years of wishing, they finally had their dog, and the children were so happy until he vomited about halfway home and then had diarrhea the remainder of our voyage of the damned.

"You wanted a dog," my wife said as she instructed the kids to roll down the windows so they wouldn't hurl.

Six months later, still a puppy, he permanently endeared himself to my wife—by trying to kill her. She'd been getting out of her car when the dog started frantically circling her, and then he apparently decided, "I'm a dog, and I want to sit on her head!" That's when he jumped up on her and knocked her over onto her kneecap, which promptly dislocated as it broke into bits.

She had four surgeries over three years; none of them worked, until the doctor who probably needed a wing on his vacation home decided it was time for total knee replacement, which should really be called total bank-account vacuuming.

Now she has a titanium knee. Her story is so painful to hear that when she recounted it to a professional grief counselor, at a New York cocktail party, the man burst into tears. Then he asked her about his girlfriend's knee, and my wife's prognosis as to whether the girlfriend would ever be able to ski again. "Maybe," said my wife, Dr. Mom.

The number one question people ask her is "Do you still have the dog?"

The answer is yes.

When you add up the initial cost of sixteen hundred dollars, along with the invisible fence, five surgeries at a very retail New York hospital, three years of physical therapy, the WD-40 to oil her knee (that's a joke), and an extensive wardrobe so that my wife's clothing matched her leg braces—"Nothing goes with crutches!"—this dog has cost us and our insurance company in excess of $327,090.

If more people knew that the answer to the question "How much is that doggie in the window?" is "More than your house," cat sales would skyrocket.

I am an expert at cats; I shared a pricey Washington, D.C., condo with one. Since we lived not far from the legendary Watergate, I named him G. Gordon Kitty. He was a pretty gray-and-white cat; whenever I'd nap, he would lie on my chest and purr in my ear. When I'd wake, I'd have an ear canal full of cat drool that would run down the side of my face the balance of the day.

He was cute, but he was mean, and wild. He'd hiss and bite, and just to make sure I understood who was boss in my two-bedroom walk-up, the day after Roche Bobois delivered a vastly overpriced white leather couch and chairs, G. Gordon ruined them by sharpening his claws on them. There were holes everywhere. Think James Caan at the tollbooth in **The Godfather**.

But Gordon wasn't just my problem. I used to have a wonderful woman who for thirty-five dollars would come into my house and make it look like I didn't live there. She did that until the day I got an urgent call from a neighbor who said she could hear Lupe screaming for help.

When I arrived, G. Gordon, who had once been a barn cat, rescued from the mean streets of Kansas, had cornered Lupe in the bathroom. Luckily for me, she was stuck in there for an hour, with nothing to do but clean it. The lavatory was sparkling, but the clean did not last forever; Lupe, quite wisely, never returned to the scene of the cat.

One day three years later, married and living in the suburbs, I got a real jolt upon arriving home. Many men love to be greeted at the door with an adult beverage and fleecy slippers. My wife handed me a five-pound soaked Pamper. "Look at this!"

Exhibit A showed that right over the spot commonly referred to as the "private area" there was one mouthful of Pamper missing. G. Gordon had taken a bite and won himself a one-way ticket to a new home. Ironically, his new owner lived in the famous Watergate apartment building, the same one that had made G. Gordon Liddy infamous. And if you've noticed, since G. Gordon Kitty has been living there, there has not been another break-in. Coincidence?

There was a fifteen-year petless span between when the cat almost neutered my son and when we got the dog that almost killed my wife and my 401(k).

I'm starting to think maybe we're not pet people.

MRS. HAPPY'S ADVICE

Pets are great companions, and if they can't be with you all the time, the fleas that jump off them onto you can be.

Your spouse won't give you unconditional love, but your dog will.

Having a pet is a great way to practice for having a baby. Pets are also very needy. Getting the dog was like having another child. There's the diet to manage, walks, vet visits, and of course dressing him up in a Halloween costume, much to his horror. "Must get devil horns off head," I knew he was thinking as he wildly swung his head back and forth until the horns hit the wall next to his $165 Orvis feeding station.

There are many differences between pet care and child care. The big one is that unlike dogs, most kids balk at drinking out of the toilet.

VOLUN-TEERS OF A CLOWN

Public Service

My wife is a great public servant. She's a CCD teacher, a class mom, a Boy and Girl Scout leader, and neighborhood watch commander, and in her spare time she's trying to feed the homeless and build a library in a children's trauma ward. I, on the other hand, am "pretty busy" from now until internment.

So she signed me up to work at a soup kitchen in Jersey City, New Jersey. They were looking for male volunteers because it was in a tough part of town. I really didn't see any downside. I'd seen television pictures on Thanksgiving of celebrities at soup kitchens, handing out turkey parts, and I thought this would be my chance to give back to humanity, while perhaps being on the same soup-line shift as Eva Longoria.

There wasn't a celebrity in the joint, but believe me, there were plenty of desperate house-wives and their children. As they lined up, it broke my heart that they had so little in life, while I had so much. "I'm happy to help," I told the woman in charge, and she immediately put me to work preparing the meal.

Few soup kitchens have state-of-the-art Vulcan appliances or appliance operator manuals. Luckily this one had the same gas stove my grandma had in her house in the 1960s, and I knew how to light it with a match. But it didn't really light, thanks to the gas leak.

Pppfptttt was followed by a white-flash **boom** reminiscent of when the Concorde used to fly above our house. That was immediately followed by a voice from the other room, "Look out for that gas leak!" The good news was that the gas that had pooled in the empty oven had just vaporized, so it couldn't hurt anybody. The bad news was it also vaporized all of my arm hair. It had been such a pretty golden blond. Now it was all singed and bent over, and on top of that, it smelled funny. Who knew that reheating meat loaf was a contact sport?

The balance of the food prep was uneventful, until about a half an hour later when I was asked by the helpful woman who had told me to look out for the gas leak to remove the corn from the oven for serving. That would be a snap. I'd been taking vegetables out of the oven since I was forty. The pot holders I used had clearly been in service for many meals. They were singed and frayed. I mention that because a piece of the decorative trim dragged across the five-hundred-degree oven floor as I pulled out the scalloped corn. It only took about two seconds for the mitt to catch fire. Earlier I'd lost all visible appendage hair, and now my only hands were engulfed in flames. You know how when you roast a marshmallow over a fire it has that flame halo? That's what I had going on with my hands, except I was holding five pounds of about-to-pop corn.

Thankfully the woman in charge knew exactly what to do when a volunteer was on fire: she threw half a sack of flour on me. (Note to EMTs: flour + burning flesh = Kentucky Fried Husband.)

"Holy smoke!" a kid from my church said.

"Yes, I am," I replied.

"How'd it go?" my wife asked when I arrived home.

"Fine" was my total response as I excused myself to my private computer to Google "fore-arm hair restoration." She didn't realize that I was a whisker away from looking like an extra in **The Mummy** until the next day as we walked into church.

"Are you okay?" a fellow volunteer asked.

"I'm fine," I said, as my fellow volunteer launched into a breathless account of how I kept working right up until I caught fire a second time while carrying ten pounds of corn that is not usually served flambéed.

From my lack of explanation, plus the Mr. Angry face, the message to my wife was clear: "I don't want to volunteer for anything unless it can be done while napping."

That was her segue. "You want to be a Boy Scout chaperone next month?" It was a dirty trick. What father wouldn't want to spend time with his son out in the woods, three days without shaving and bathing, charring meat items to the point where you'd need a coroner. "It's a T-bone, son, eat around the charcoal."

"Sure," I said, making a mental note to stay at least seventy-five feet from the campfire at all times.

"Terrific," she said approvingly.

"Am I **already** signed up?"

"Last Tuesday."

She was good.

Unlike my previous bout with public service, this time I did not spontaneously combust at any point, because torrential rains washed out the first eighteen hours. Briefly the sun shined, and many of the dads retired to the soaking pup tents for naps.

"Dad, there's a BEAR!" was not what I was expecting to hear from my son, who I'd presumed was napping next to me in the tent. I unzipped the bug screen and bolted out in time to see the back of my son's blond head as he was running **toward** a two-hundred-pound black bear, which was there thanks to the idiot father who had snuck a dozen Dunkin' Donuts to the campsite, despite the sign BEAR, EVERYWHERE, DON'T BRING FOOD!

Just before my son got to the bear, a Scout leader emerged from his tent with a wooden spoon and a tin pot, and began banging on the pot. And just like in the movies, the bear stopped snacking and started running toward the Girl Scout camp down the road. Hide the Thin Mints, girls!

On the last night, things dried out, there were no more **Wild Kingdom** moments, and I wound up having a nice chat with one of the other dads, a very successful stockbroker. "Confidentially, I'm having my best year **ever,**" he told me with italics in his voice. After a little coaxing, I finally wore him down and he gave me the name of a secret stock that was making him tons of money.

That following Monday, I went online at nine-thirty eastern time and hitched my wagon to that money-making supernova-stock pick, investing as much as I could. The stock was Enron, and two days later, it tanked.

Why did that bear eat the doughnuts, and not me?

MRS. HAPPY'S ADVICE

Volunteering cannot only help make this a better world; it can strengthen that marriage bond. However, if you're going to be a couple, then you should volunteer to do things together.

And since women generally spend more time in the kitchen, they should probably light the stove, as the men-folk stand in the background plugging their ears waiting for the boom!

As for my personal history, it's always worth it, despite the cost. What does it cost, you ask? Just remember, I can't say "volunteers" without "tears."

GOOD SPORTS

Playing Together

I'm looking in the mirror. White shoes, white socks, white shorts, and white shirt.

I'm not the Man from Glad, I'm playing couples tennis. It's our first Friday night under the lights, playing tennis with a half a dozen married friends. The concept is simple: hit some balls, have some laughs, and arrive home ninety seconds before the babysitter starts paging you.

Great premise, but in real life, once you walk out onto the field of combat, your friends turn into wild animals who will do whatever it takes to win even if that means gutting you like a trout with their bare hands.

I am by my own admission not a good player, which is abundantly apparent to all who stand across the net from me. It takes just a few minutes of observation to see that the best way for the opposing team to win is to hit the ball to me.

Luckily, my wife is an amazing tennis player; she can zoom all over the court and make me look respectable. And after the first few months we were unbeaten. As the final tournament, held on actual clay courts, approached, we sensed a sea change. The other husband-wife combos, who'd played at this country club for years before they invited us to join their fun, didn't like having the newcomers winning. That's when they apparently changed their strategy from "Let's just have fun" to "Kill them NOW!"

Welcome to the War on Tennis

The gloves first came off when a business executive who called in sick to work for a week because of recent elbow surgery showed up for our Friday-night court date shot full of cortisone. My wife felt sorry for him—after all, he'd taken off an arm sling just to play—and tried to shoot around him so he wouldn't get hurt more.

But he and his wife were not our friends at that moment; they'd turned into savage killing machines, and toward the end of the game, with us leading, they changed their game plan. The man with the bad elbow moved up to the net and started hitting the ball as hard as he could, skirt level at my wife. She whacked it right back at him time after time. It bugged me that this weenie would go after my wife, but she could handle herself, so I wasn't worried about her. I should have been worried about me.

Just a serve away from a win, he illegally poached the ball over the net and drilled it straight into my face. It hit so hard, the impact knocked me over backward. I scraped my elbows bloody and ripped two inches of skin off my knees. One inch south, and I'd be wearing a patch these days and my daughter would be saying, "Daddy's a pirate!" I should have burst into tears, but I didn't want to get my tennis whites wet. They were already bloody, and I didn't know if my wife had enough OxiClean to save them. She ran over to tend to the wounded, but the assassin and his wife returned to their game positions.

"What are you doing?" I asked the perpetrator from my fully reclined position.

No response.

"There is no bleeding in tennis! Looky, I'm bloody!"

Pause. Finally a meager "You don't think I did that on purpose, do you?" he volleyed across the net.

"Yes," I shot back, giving him the stink eye.

"Whatever. You gonna play or just lie there and bleed?"

We played and **lost.** There was nary a word after the match—no socializing, no fake kiss, no nothing. We were seething when we hopped into my wife's SUV and she drove me to the emergency room for a tetanus shot, because I wasn't in enough pain yet.

The following Friday, a formerly lovely couple from California faced off against us in the play-offs. Apparently they'd heard that shooting at my head was a surefire way to win. Both the husband **and** the wife launched shot after shot directly at my brainpan. It was like playing tennis with Mr.

and Mrs. Saddam Hussein. I generally stepped aside and let my partner return them from the backfield. But when the guy just missed me with the same shot that had taken me out the week before, my wife got that look that I know means "It's time to take out the trash."

Using her racquet like a bazooka, she sent a fuzzy ball directly and surgically into the husband's private area.

"**Aaaarrrrrggg!**" He went down. Other couples around us, who were not in our league but knew his reputation, stopped to savor the moment. He slowly stood up, but he should have stayed down—the red clay dust from the ball left no doubt where the ball had made contact with Mr. Tough Guy.

We dropped out of the league when we moved from that state. Now, many years later, we're learning how to golf. It's just me versus my wife. Remembering she's a crack shot, when she's teeing off I stand **behind** her, with my legs crossed, waiting for an invitation to the nineteenth hole.

MR. HAPPY'S ADVICE

If you're ever asked to play in a couples league, insist that no score be kept. Make it like T-ball, where it's always a tie.

The only game that you should do everything you can to win is strip poker.

OUR MARRIAGE IS PERFECT, LET'S DATE!

An Experiment

How many times have you heard that there's somebody waiting out there who is just perfect for each one of us? The problem is figuring out who they are, where they are, how you will meet them, and which outfit will make you look thin when you do.

I'm lucky, I found mine. My wife and I both believe we were meant to be together. But why should we trust an intuition, when we could let modern technology declare us officially perfect? So to celebrate our twentieth anniversary, we joined an online dating club.

Nothing says "I love you" more than throwing your happily married hats into the dating database of hundreds of thousands of single men who are so desperate for love they'd be happy to crowbar my wife away from me. Of course we were not looking for a date; we wanted to see how meant for each other we were according to a computer program. That's how these dating services work. You fill out a lengthy questionnaire—likes and dislikes, et cetera—that profiles your personality, and then the computer spits out a long list of great matches. We hoped the computer would confirm that I was the best person for her, and vice versa.

I asked my wife if she thought that twenty years ago we'd have found each other if we'd used an online dating site, had they existed back then. "No," she said. "I don't generally fall for cheap control freaks." She's a real kidder.

And thus started our odyssey. We didn't join one of the really big companies, instead using a free site that boasted several hundred thousand sets of eyeballs. Who cared if those eyeballs belonged to people who weren't paying for a service? For our purposes it would be just fine to go fishing in this database of fellow cheapskates. Over the course of several days, we filled out the questionnaires. We did this individually, while the kids were at school, because there's something unnerving to a seventh-grader about seeing her mother answering flirty questions on the same computer the daughter uses for social studies.

Important Disclosure: We were not 100 percent truthful. We both told the same lie—that we were single. Oddly, the club wouldn't let married people go fishing. My wife told one additional fib—that her highest level of education was graduate school. Apparently she didn't want to get stuck with a doofus. I mean **another** doofus.

The great thing about joining one of these clubs is that as soon as you finish answering all of the questions, all you have to do is push a button and you get to see the faces of your best chances at love. I was expecting to be the first name on her list. Sadly, I was not, so we moved on to the next. Nope. We searched her fifty-three pages, and I was nowhere to be found. Out of a database of several hundred thousand, I was not in her top 532 of **local** men. These weren't guys who lived in Barcelona; these were local guys, who, according to the computer, were a better match. Let's meet a few.

- A twenty-four-year-old in Poughkeepsie who said his three favorite things are women, tattoos, and cars.
- A man from Yonkers whose greatest achievement was drinking a forty-ounce Budweiser in eight minutes. "It's a record that still stands."
- A guy who said his favorite pastime was "spanking."

Stunned, we opened up my account. I was sure my wife had done something wrong on her questionnaire, but I'd done mine by the book, and I was positive she would be on the first page of matches.

She wasn't. I looked for almost an hour, and she wasn't in my top 676 local matches. Rather than hook me up with a woman who lived **at my address,** the computer paired me with women who lived as far as two states away. For gas conservation and carpooling purposes alone my wife and I should have been matched up.

Instead of my wife, the computer said I should be dating

- "Laurenchiladas," a woman who thought it was clever to contract her name with a popular Mexican comfort food.
- A woman who described herself as a "singer, songwriter, astronaut." Is Sally Ride on the market?
- "Jenny," who wrote, "I have the cutest nose in the world." (Oddly, the profile picture is of only a single lock of her hair.) She also wrote, "My wrists are tattooed in Latin"; so clearly she was looking to pick up an altar boy.

These were not the results we were expecting. Suddenly there was a wisp of wonder in both of us. "Maybe we've been married for two decades to **the wrong person!**" The next time my wife was late, my paranoid gland would kick in and I'd imagine she was on the phone with "Al-chemist" (one of her matches), who wrote that he spent a lot of time thinking about "what I had for breakfast." Or maybe she was chatting up the teacher in White Plains who sold himself by writing, "My smile and eyes draw people to me."

I now have a profound understanding of what online dating can do. It can give you a scientific statistic (87 percent) of how closely your answers match somebody else's. Then of course you've got to make contact and see if there's a spark of some sort. Online dating is a wonderful tool for the person who wants to see all the options out there, and the questionnaire eliminates scads of people who are simply **wrong** for you.

So why did the computer say other people were a better match for us than each other?

There are three possibilities.

1. The site was a complete scam.
2. My wife and I have different answers to life's big questions. She says "Paper," I say "Plastic."
3. The woman I live with is not the woman I married. My original bride has been kidnapped sometime over the last twenty years and a woman who underwent painful plastic surgery to look like her, because she was out for the hundreds of dollars in my family fortune, has taken her place.

If the latter is true, it leads me to just two logical questions: "Where is my **real** wife?" And "Until I find her, can I still claim a standard deduction on my 1040 for **two** women? My real wife and the look-alike?"

WARNING: Married people should not online-date. For a small investment of time and money, your spouse can obtain the scientific knowledge that there are **other** people out there who are a better match than you are.

Sir Francis Bacon famously observed, "Knowledge is power," but in this case I'd rather be in the dark. Actually, I'd rather have the bacon.

chapter four

Kids

GROWING YOUR FAMILY TREE

What Are You In For?

Welcome to the long and winding road that is parenthood. During the next fifty years, you will spend a good portion of each day worried about **everything.** Is this the right baby shampoo? What part of the worm did he eat? And if my child is not home yet, is it because he's doing drugs or at a cockfight gambling away his birthday money from Grandma?

Becoming a parent is the greatest single event of your life. It is the best thing that's ever happened to me. My wife feels the same way. But be wary, it's the hardest job you'll ever have. It's hard to convince your sixteen-year-old son to take his foot off the gas as he takes a corner at forty-five miles an hour, and it's tricky negotiating with a teenage daughter about why she really shouldn't go out in public in a skirt the length of a beer cozy, but she insists, and winds up looking like your family's youngest prostitute. Theoretically it would be easier to teach a spaniel how to change the spark plugs on your Honda than to raise a child through the age of innocence.

Despite the many rolls of Tums you'll suck down as your children grow, they will say things that make you smile, do things to make you cry, and not allow you to get one full night of sleep again until they enroll in a college that you could never get in to, and that your family really can't afford.

In the early days, they'll just lie there and expect to be fed, clothed, and sanitized after going potty the same way our Apollo astronauts did. Then one day they'll be ready to leave the house and go to school, where despite your careful parenting, peer pressure can vaporize it all faster than you can say "Dude, pass the Coors."

"Mom," my high school senior son said, "the girls' swim team wants me to meet them for dinner."

"Where?" my wife cross-examined.

"Hooters," he said with a straight face (and racing heart).

"No," she said as she realized she'd missed the deadline for homeschooling.

As your family grows, you will discover that while you spent thousands of dollars processing pictures of your first child's every move, and videotaping most of her first two years in real time, when your last child rolls around, the novelty of chronicling every move has long worn off, and when you're called upon to produce a current photo of your youngest, the best you can find is their school picture or a surveillance tape from a Wal-Mart parking lot.

Our kids kept our house in a perpetual state of disorganization and chaos. Every parent gets the urgent "There's a hairy kid-eating monster in my closet!" My favorite wildlife encounter was during a fishing trip when I asked my son and his friend to search for night crawlers, and shortly they returned gleeful that they'd found a big juicy one. They had trouble and asked me for help. "Daddy, come here." That's when I discovered they were trying to bait their hook with a live water moccasin.

From the day you return from the hospital with your Pampers-wearing, Similac-sucking bundle of joy, older parents will say, "Enjoy them while you can, they grow up so fast." I personally used to think, "Don't worry about me, Pops, I'm **young!**"

I've now blinked my eyes and one is in college, one is in high school (wearing eye makeup), and my baby is cross-examining my wife about the global implications of the Central American Free Trade Act. It seems like it was last Tuesday that she was four, hysterically laughing in the bathroom. My wife went in to see what was so funny, and there she stood with her Barney drawers around her ankles, bare-butted and bent over the bowl, squealing, "Look! My poopy is smiling!" It wasn't actually smiling, but it was bent like a smile. She asked if we could take a picture of it, but we declined due to a strict family rule of not photographing bowel movements.

I have 125,749 stories of cuteness. They are tempered by the 347,687 incidents that fall into the "forget as quickly as possible" category.

And yet, I wouldn't have it any other way.

In the end the kind of child you raise is the kind of person who will either pay to get you into a fancy assisted living home in Boca Raton or discreetly inquire whether euthanasia programs are included in your Medicaid coverage.

PEE ON THE STICK

Pregnancy

Kids are wonderful people you can actually create with things you have around the house.

"My skirt is tight," my wife said.

"You want me to yell at the dry cleaner?" I asked.

"I think I'm pregnant, you idiot!"

You've heard that hormones change a woman's personality when she's pregnant, right? It's

WHAT KIND OF PARENT ARE YOU?

	Traditional	Modern	Totalitarian	Clueless
YOUR HISTORICAL ROLE MODELS?	Ozzie and Harriet	The parents on **The OC**	The Stalins	Homer and Marge Simpson
DISCIPLINE TECHNIQUE	Spanking	Time-out	Gulag	Forcing kids to watch bowling
PET PEEVES	Muddy tracks in kitchen	Family blog not updated	Kids didn't refill ammo dump	When your kids forget your name
SCHOOL	Ivy League	Home	Military	(Absent)

	Traditional	Modern	Totalitarian	Clueless
DOG'S NAME	Lassie	Bjork	Glock	What dog?
FAVORITE PASTIME	Bridge	Listening to iPod	Wallpapering the Panic Room	Draining Beer Miser
GREATEST ACHIEVEMENT	Child to Harvard	Carb-free lasagne	Built own barbecue/bunker	Garbage put out last night
WHAT YOU SAY TO YOUR KIDS THE MOST	Stop it.	Please stop.	Stop or I'll shoot.	What kids?

true, but you didn't hear it from me. I made the mistake early in my wife's first pregnancy of asking this question while shopping for affordable Swedish furniture at Ikea: "Are your hormones raging?" She burst into tears. Being a rookie father-to-be, I didn't realize that "Are your hormones raging?" is translated by a mother-to-be as "Honey, you're being a psycho right now, but it's okay, you're pregnant."

I made that mistake one time only.

Her first trimester was ninety days of sheer agony, for both of us. The morning sickness was overwhelming. After a routine visit to her ob-gyn, she double-parked her car and ran into a grocery store to buy something for dinner. Somewhere over by the meat case, she developed the overwhelming urge to puke. But knowing she'd never be able to cash a check there again if she hurled near the lamb chops, she dashed out of the store, then threw up in front of a cop who was writing a ticket for her double-parked vehicle.

"Lady," the cop said, "it's not that bad, it's just a ticket."

Luckily the exact day she transitioned from first to second trimester, she got her appetite back, thanks to her sumo gene kicking in. One night at two-thirty I woke to the sound of the smoke detector in the kitchen going crazy. I raced downstairs with a fire extinguisher ready to put out a three-alarmer, when I saw my wife was putting the final touches on a bacon, lettuce, and tomato sandwich. She'd burned the bacon, and that set off the alarm. "Don't give me a hard time," she said, "I'm eating for two."

"Who, you and Shaq?"

During this time we spent our leisure hours "nesting," finding baby furniture and other expensive stuff we'd use once and throw away. She'd heard of an Italian state-of-the-art stroller she had to have. Over a series of weekends we drove through three states until we found one—the last one available in the 202, 301, and 703 area codes. It was the floor model; and it didn't have any of the instructions or the box.

"We'll take it," my wife told the clerk, sensing that another woman who was "shopping for two" was stalking it. The maternal instinct was so strong that nothing would stand between my wife and the baby buggy. At our station wagon I immediately recognized the problem with not having instructions; we couldn't figure out how to collapse the damn thing. After twenty minutes of frustration I threw it into the trunk uncollapsed and tied down the rear hatch so it was 75 percent closed. The pregnant lady I was married to burst into tears. By now I knew it was the hormones talking, so I distracted her with the one line that I'd learned would stop crying jags dead in their tracks nine out of ten times.

"How about Taco Bell?"

A smile appeared, and so did a coupon, and soon we were pulling up to the drive-through window for a predinner snack. I, my wife, and our dining companion, Shaquille O'Neal.

MRS. HAPPY'S ADVICE

The husband can't really identify with what a pregnant woman is going through, unless he has at some point had another person embedded in his gut kicking the soup out of his spleen while trying to make a jailbreak. So it's critical that he does whatever it takes to make his not-so-little lady comfortable. "Hello, I'm your husband, and I'll be your waiter for the next four months."

IMPORTANT POINT: If you have any medical concerns or questions, talk to the appropriate doctor. I heard a story about one pregnant woman who went to her ob-gyn's office for a routine exam and asked at the conclusion, "My husband wants to know if **it** is still all right?"

The doctor apparently heard this question all the time and assured her, "Sex is okay until late in the third trimester."

Embarrassed, she said, "I'm not talking about sex; he wants to know if I can still mow the yard."

She could.

DIAL M FOR MOTHER

Delivery Day

I was born after my mother went through a thigh-numbing thirty-six hours of labor. The next day her doctor volunteered to go on an eighteen-month tour of duty on the hospital ship the SS **Hope**. Apparently the hope of curing malaria and typhoid fever in a Third World country where the only taste of modern life was powdered milk would be a walk in the park compared to the day and a half of sweating and squeezing from my mother.

In the final moments of my delivery, the doctor sensed something was going wrong and gave Mother Nature a helping hand. To this day, next to my left eye I have a tiny scar where the doctor dragged me into this world with a set of stainless-steel forceps that looked like jumbo salad tongs. My father wasn't in the delivery room when I was born—or in the waiting room either. He wasn't even on the same continent. He was wearing the uniform of a private in the United States Army, based in Europe. A telegram informed him that he had a son, as he proudly stood guard in Stuttgart, Germany, just to make sure Mercedes-Benz employees didn't try anything crazy like taking over the world.

I, on the other hand, would not only be in the same room with my wife, I would be her labor and delivery coach. So for months we'd jumped from one church basement to another, attending natural-childbirth classes. To some, natural childbirth means not using drugs. To my wife, natural childbirth is when the woman doesn't wear makeup.

On her first D Day, we arrived at George Washington University Hospital, the same place where they took President Reagan after John Hinckley revealed his fascination with Jodie Foster to the world. We punched in predawn, but it wasn't until dark that the contractions were coming at the appropriate interval and the nurse told us to start the Lamaze breathing.

"Pant, blow, pant, blow," I instructed. And just like Pavlov's wife, she followed my instruction; she panted and blew, panted and blew, for more than an hour. Our labor instructor said that during delivery "the woman easily overheats," so she advised that the husband (me) spray Evian mist lightly on her face. I sprayed away as my wife panted and blew. After half an hour of misting, it looked like I'd been spraying her with Pam; she was sweaty and wet, and despite its intended calming effect, she was ready to strangle me—it would have been justifiable husband-icide.

"Stop with the water, I'm drowning here."

So I shifted into my golf voice and did some play-by-play announcing of the peaks and valleys of pain that the contraction monitor was showing. "Oh this is going to be a big one," I warned, and it was. "How much does it hurt?" I asked in that "I care" voice.

"Like I'm passing a golf cart." She was now dry again but still panting and blowing, panting and blowing, when she made a stunning admission. "This breathing thing isn't working. Gimme an epidural, NOW!"

"Could you try the breathing a little longer, hon?" the nurse coaxed.

"NOW!"

An hour later it was time to have the baby, but the baby wasn't ready for his debut. His heart rate had slowed, and the doctor said something about the baby being "stuck." There was a flurry of activity, and then forty-five seconds later, just as I was delivered thirty years earlier; my son arrived courtesy of giant salad tongs.

"Wwwwwhaaaaaaaaaa!"

"It's a boy!" the doctor pronounced. He'd asked me if I wanted to stand behind the nurse for a good angle of the head crowning, but I declined. When would I show that tape, at his high school graduation? I can just image what the voice-over would sound like…"And here he is coming out of the birth canal. His mother did a great job—that's some good-looking placenta!"

I did videotape his first fifteen minutes breathing on his own, from a tasteful angle, and I got the moment his blue body was placed under a heat lamp. Wearing a knit stocking cap, he looked like either a rapper or a future convenience-store armed robber.

"Do you want to cut the cord?" the doctor asked me.

Was he kidding? But I didn't want to appear nonmacho at this delicate time, so I decided to scare him into doing it himself.

"I'd love to," I said, "but only if I can use a chain saw."

Snip clipped the doctor.

They say that with each child the birth is easier, and I've found that to be true. However, with each birth things got weirder. Three years later, my wife was back in the saddle again. In those three short years the medical community had made a huge improvement in pain management, and she was instructed that "any time you feel a crimp or a cramp, just push this button," and the nurse showed her a gizmo that would send a powerful narcotic directly into her backside through an epidural needle. The device looked like it was from Nintendo. We called it her "Painboy."

After fifty K-2s on the contraction monitor, Painboy was out of juice.

Then the nurse explained that after a certain number of button pushes in an hour, "nothing comes out." She politely asked my wife to push the button only when the pain was truly overwhelming.

"**Aaaaaaahhhha!** Somebody HELP ME!" It was hard to miss the weeper being rushed into the adjacent delivery room. Misery loves company, but this company was screaming at the top of her lungs.

"God it hurts! Please help me...ANYBODY!" My wife locked eyes with the nurse. "I'm glad I'm in here and not in **that** room."

"**Aaaaaaahhhha!** Somebody get this thing out of me!"

It reminded me of Monica Seles grunting and groaning every time she returned a volley at the U.S. Open.

"I'll buy her an epidural," I said to our nurse, "if she'll shut up."

"That freakin' !@#$ who did this to me is &;cr%$ dead!"

This was what it must sound like when a pregnant Teamster delivers a forklift through the birth canal. Suddenly my wife's imminent childbearing seemed so humdrum. I wanted to go see what was happening next door. So I nodded to my wife, who gave me the "Sure, go, I'll have your baby—you go visit Mrs. Andrew Dice Clay."

I immediately noted one difference between my wife's room and the bigmouthed momma's, and I was a little envious. We didn't have armed guards. A male county sheriff's officer was standing at the door; a female officer stood next to the screecher creature. Who was it? I wondered. A celebrity? A high-ranking government official? A diplomat?

"She's a prisoner," our nurse whispered upon my return. Terrific. All we wanted was another uneventful birth, and instead we were being held hostage by a woman who was living the Folsom Prison Blues.

"Sometimes a woman who's just about to have a baby will go into a store and shoplift," the nurse continued, "knowing she'll get caught."

"Why is that?"

"Because they don't have health insurance. But if you're in the custody of the county at the time of your birth, you get a free delivery, thanks to the local jail."

"Why don't they give her a Painboy, so she's not screaming?" I asked.

"She's probably a heroin addict," the nurse said. "That lady's got stronger stuff than we do in her purse!"

A few minutes earlier I had really thought the bigmouth next door was a jerk. Now I felt like the dope. This was just another example of what lengths a mother will go to to take care of her kids, even to the point of getting arrested and probably convicted of a felony, just so her baby can start life in a nice, clean hospital. Her screaming lasted until her voice was replaced by that of her baby girl's.

Our baby girl arrived shortly after midnight, dodging a Halloween birth and instead being born on All Saints Day.

By the time our third child came along, much of the pregnancy prep magic was gone. We'd given up on Lamaze in favor of Le Mans, as in 24 Hours of Le Mans, and instead of controlled breathing, we planned to just drive fast to the hospital, where a reliable nursing staff would hook my wife to a narcotic lifeline and wake me when the baby arrived. For our final birth we chose a hospital that was less **St. Elsewhere,** more Hyatt. Our room looked like a suite in a fine hotel. It was carpeted, had a huge couch, a big television, even a refrigerator stocked with sandwiches for me.

"Go find the nurse and tell her my water broke," my wife said, interrupting an important report I was monitoring on **Entertainment Tonight.**

I went to the nurse's station, where they seemed to be bummed out that they'd have to go to work. A nurse came in, asked my wife how she was, then pushed a button on the side of the bed, whereupon the bed transformed into a birthing station. Out of the side popped stainless-steel stirrups. Five minutes later her doctor appeared. This doctor had an eight o'clock dinner reservation at a nearby Japanese steak house, and after a full day of baby birthing, she was starving.

"I'm going to speed this up," she said, as she put on a rubber glove and stuck her hand into the delicate birth zone. I have no idea what she did, but apparently she found the factory-installed release hatch, because five minutes after she'd put on the glove, my wife was fully dilated from her previous 30 percent, and five pushes later a baby was born, a cord was cut (by a professional), and the doctor arrived at her dinner reservation in time for the miso soup.

SORRY, TALLULAH'S TAKEN

Naming the Baby

Most of us will never have our names emblazoned upon a hospital wing, a university building, or a major thoroughfare; the best we'll ever do is put the name of our choice on a child. There are many things to consider when selecting a name that will fit for a lifetime.

If we named our children by how they looked at birth, the kindergartens of the world would be filled with Winstons, Quasimodos, and Camillas (as in Parker Bowles).

Clearly other criteria must be used.

My wife and I discussed our children's names for months. She has a friend who'd named his children after characters in important works of literature. Brilliant! Why didn't we think of that first? We too wanted something one-of-a-kind. But the literature department had already been harvested. For months we'd scrutinize every off-beat word as a possible name. In the beginning we test-drove names from the world of fashion. Corduroy, Flannel, and Calico were all considered momentarily before we sobered up. "Satin sounds like a stripper," my wife said, pooh-poohing my suggestion.

Then we considered animal names, but after we couldn't find a good middle name for Lemur, we moved to the Great Masters. "How about Leonardo?"

"Lenny?" She instantly thought **Laverne & Shirley** as my dream of a Da Vinci in the house was derailed.

Driving through Manhattan, it hit me. Name them after a place! A destination. As we drove down an avenue famous for advertising, I looked up at a street sign and inspiration struck. "What about Madison?"

"Streets," my wife replied, "don't make good kids names."

"Then how about SoHo?"

"His friends will call him Ho."

"It worked for Ho Chi Minh."

The idea of a place seemed like a good one. We had a friend who had a son named Montana, and since that was taken, we scanned a Rand McNally atlas like fifth-graders cramming for a social studies test, until we hit pay dirt. There, in the heart of Tennessee, was our name.

"What about Memphis?"

"Memphis…"

There was something there. Memphis was the name of a style of popular design (bright, kitschy, playful). It was also a name from Greek mythology. And of course a famous city in the heartland that was home for a terrific style of barbecue. We loved Memphis. It was different from every other kid's name, but it was a hard sell to friends and family.

"You've never even **been** to Memphis!" my mother said in that voice that told me she was about to get in the car and drive to my house to administer an at-home drug test.

"But, Mom—"

"You're from Kansas! Would you name your child Topeka?"

"Of course not, that's stupid—"

"So's Memphis," she said as she concluded our phone call with a click.

You can't fight Memphis City Hall. Time to move to current events. The biggest story of the summer of our baby's birth was that Halley's comet was coming. It zooms by only once every seventy-six years. It was a divine sign. So we decided right then and there. Her name would be Halley.

Perfect. It was a done deal, until the sonogram. Our baby girl was a boy. Boys generally aren't named Halley. (Haley Joel Osment's parents were trailblazers.)

The doctor suggested shortening Halley to Hal. But I couldn't get the image of Hal from **2001: A Space Odyssey** out of my head.

In the end we decided to pick the name of a saint. There were plenty to choose from, and my mother couldn't argue about somebody who's got a holy name.

Our first son was named Peter.

Then the second baby arrived, and the process was trickier. What name would go with our last name and have a complimentary connection to her brother's name?

Back on Saint Street, we chose Mary.

With our third and last child, we faced the greatest dilemma: If it was a boy, we wanted to name him after Saint Paul, but then our children's names would be Peter, Paul, and Mary. Suddenly a branch of our family tree was on the verge of looking like a sixties folk trio.

"Are you out of your mind?" my wife said.

My dream of a Peter, Paul and Mary was dashed with the arrival of a girl. "You can't name her Paul," my relieved wife said with a smile.

"How about Paula?"

"Stop it."

"Mrs. Paul's?"

"That's taken."

In the end, when the nurse arrived and asked the name, Sally was written on the line. It wasn't a saint's name; it wasn't a family name. It did have the right number of syllables to match the last name. It had come down to one thing: when we first saw her, she **looked** like a Sally.

That Christmas, to commemorate the completion of our family, I went to a fancy jewelry store and had the initials of the children my wife brought into this world engraved on a sterling-silver bracelet.

The names Peter, Mary, and Sally were shortened to their initials: "P-M-S."

I got a funny trio after all.

MRS. HAPPY'S ADVICE

You can never go wrong naming a kid after a family member. Unless that family member is Sammy "the Bull" Gravano.

Short names are less likely to get butchered.

Make names easy to remember.

Nothing bothers children more than when you confuse their names. I

call Mary Sally or Sally Mary at least three times a week. I also call Peter Mary, and that's a problem for a boy who's just recently started shaving, with his aunt's Lady Norelco.

If you think you need extra credit on your account to assure you'll get into heaven, you can't go wrong with a saint's name. Those of you on the bubble should consider Matthew or Teresa over Billy or Brandi.

BREAST INTENTIONS

Feeding in Public

On the boob tube on May 17, 2005, Barbara Walters recounted to her coffee-guzzling cohosts that she'd been jetting somewhere and was surprised when the mother next to her popped her top and started nursing her child. "It made me very nervous," she said in that Barbara Walters voice.

An avalanche of publicity followed, and a tiny group of "lactivists" called for a "nurse-in" to protest her comment. Why were the lactivists up in arms about this, and not the least bit concerned that I'm lactose-intolerant?

To be honest, when my wife was breast-feeding our kids in public places—she spent a good portion of our first ten years of marriage discreetly feeding throughout the greater metropolitan District of Columbia—it made me nervous. "Hey, what are you looking at, buddy? That's **my wife!**"

One of our first trips out of the house with our first child was for dinner at the legendary Palm restaurant in Washington, D.C. We had our son in the stroller, pulled right up to the table. It always happened after we ordered but before the food arrived: he woke up mad. Quickly the whining turned into flat-out screaming. Heads turned, and powerful congressional types gave us that same look you level at people who refer to sorbet as "sherbet."

Babies of this age have very few needs, and my wife knew it was probably time to open up the dairy-barn doors. She was not comfortable doing that at the table, so she excused herself to the coatroom. At first she tried a diaper change, just in case. No problem there. So she opened up, and surprise, he wasn't hungry. I could hear his screams from table 52, so after I finished my side salad with Russian dressing, I went to assist the little lady.

"Shhhhhhhhh!" didn't work. And neither did "I'll give you a dollar!" which used to work on my sisters. Three minutes into the howl fest, we're both on our knees in the coatroom, Shhhhhhh-ing and bouncing, when behind us we heard two patrons offer the following assessment of our kid's screamapalooza.

"There is nothing as beautiful as the sound of a baby crying."

We were facing the other direction so we couldn't see who said it, and they couldn't see my wife and I rolling our eyes at their observation. At precisely that time, Mr. Bigmouth shut up. Crisis averted, we quickly picked up the boy and stood, only to turn and come face-to-face with Angie Dickinson and Larry King. She was the one who said that the sound of a baby crying is beautiful. Larry King was probably just thinking, "I'm out with Angie Dickinson, somebody look at me!"

After some small talk about babies, they left via taxi, as did my wife, who couldn't take the scrutiny of the glaring K Streeters on expense account. She closed up her brassiere and took the baby home. I sat at our table alone and finished both New York strips.

On other occasions in public, when it was clearly time for a feeding, my wife would scan the room and find the spot with the least foot traffic. Then she'd turn away from the majority of people, open up, attach the child to the nozzle, and cover up with a baby blanket. Once during a shopping trip, they made a snack stop. She'd just plopped a slice of pizza in front of the three-year-old and started feeding the newborn in a cone of silence over by a Cinnabon. Everything worked fine for about a minute, until the three-year-old brother started to choke on the cheese. The multitasking mom knew this lifesaving technique would require both hands, so she placed the baby down, jumped to the aid of the choker, and deftly used her little finger like a hook to drag the killer **queso** out of his throat.

She saved his life. Thank goodness she was there. At that moment, the food court burst into approval applause. At the first sound of choking, many eyewitnesses turned their attention to the mother and her kids. But were they clapping because of her quick thinking or because during the cheese-ectomy, she'd placed the nursing baby in the stroller without buttoning up her blouse, which means she stood there for thirty seconds completely exposed, flashing the thoroughly entertained diners at the Galleria food court?

MRS. HAPPY'S ADVICE

Angie Dickinson, who will always be Sergeant Pepper Anderson to me, was right—there is nothing as beautiful as the sound of a baby crying. And there's nothing as beautiful as a mother nursing her child. But what's beautiful for me may freak out others. I am pro-breast-feeding. It's cheap, it's good for the kid, and just like Wendy's, the drive-through is always open. But because it is such an intimate act, it

is perhaps best if the feeder covers up as much as possible. You don't want to suffocate the child, but you don't want the businessman next to you on the train to hyperventilate either.

The last thing you want is to have some guy stare at you as you nurse and then when you're done, walk over and wedge a five-dollar tip in your Snugli.

FEAR FACTOR

Baby Monitoring

"Wwwwaaaaaaaaaaaahhhhhh!"

The baby monitor was transmitting with crystal clarity a real bloodcurdler. And it couldn't have come at a worse time—I had just poured my first cup of coffee. You could tell that we were now veteran parents, because we didn't jump up the instant he started wailing, we let him wail away awhile, just in case he cried himself back to sleep.

"Ya-ya-ya-ya-ya!"

Okay, it was my turn. I went downstairs, quietly whipped open his door, and there he was, asleep. I **knew** he'd fall asleep again, so I went back up, and just as I reached the top of the stairs, **"Ya-ya-ya-waaaaaaa!"**

My wife gave me that "I birthed him, you can burp him" look, and I turned to go back downstairs, when we heard the scariest thing of our adult lives come over our baby monitor. Sure, the baby was still howling, but there was a new voice there—that of a woman!

"It's all right, honey…"

It was one of those Stephen King moments of absolute terror. We took the steps three at a time. Flinging the door open, expecting to see a kidnapper or a Good Samaritan who slipped in through the window to help us with child care, we were shocked to see that he was alone and sound asleep.

I searched for the baby monitor and discovered that it was unplugged. Wait a minute…Taking a page from the Duane "Dog" Chapman handbook, I processed the information at hand. The transmitter down here had been unplugged. That meant that upstairs we were listening to… **somebody else's** baby! Mystery solved, fade to credits.

We figured out that these monitors were basically all on the same frequency. So if our transmitter next to the crib was off but our receiver upstairs was on, we'd hear any other baby monitors in the neighborhood. We had just heard the voice of a nearby mother comforting her child.

At first we felt like we were invading somebody's privacy. But then we realized that this device was legally licensed by the FCC, so we had the official approval of the federal government to listen in on the neighbors. Forget about ethics—we were severely sleep-deprived. Combine that with the fact that we didn't have cable television in our building and our entertainment options were limited, so listening in on the neighbors became a regular part of our day. If our baby was awake and nearby, **off** went the transmitter, and **on** went our receiver. This was better than any soap opera, because it was real!

Who is that baby? Where is its mommy? We had many questions without answers. So we made up names and backstories for the voices. We believed that the baby was a girl with an advanced set of lungs. Because she was so good at crying for an extended period, we named her Baby Jessica, after the baby made famous for being rescued live on cable television after she fell down a well in Midland, Texas.

We turned the baby monitor on early one Sunday and didn't hear the baby, but we did hear two adults about to engage in some frisky adult behavior, so we turned it off again. No wonder Jessica fell down that well—her parents left her alone while they fulfilled their caveman urges. We named her parents Fred and Wilma, as in Flintstone.

As with so many leisure activities, we eventually got bored listening to the other family change diapers and burp the baby, because we were doing it live ourselves with our own, and the thrill of listening to the same stuff on a citizens band–quality device had worn off—until my wife mentioned that she thought she'd seen a family with a baby about the age we estimated Baby Jessica to be. She'd seen them go into the apartment building directly across the street.

Now we had faces to connect to the voices. Then it dawned on us, if we could hear them, they could hear us. (They would have figured it out faster on **CSI: Schenectady,** but remember, we were sleep-deprived.) If we were listening to them, why shouldn't they listen to us?

That's when we made the crazy decision to make our lives worth eavesdropping on. We'd put on a show! Of course we had no idea if anybody else could hear through our baby monitor, but we were under the influence of Similac fumes and desperate for fun. In the beginning we produced a simple radio-style show with us sitting around the monitor as if it were a microphone, talking to our baby. We called each other different names to conceal our true identities. If the baby-monitor police busted in one morning, we wanted plausible deniability.

"Sorry, Officer, there is no person in this house by the name of Wheezy Joe."

Then we kicked it up a notch, adding plot twists and complicated story lines during baby-monitor sweeps weeks. We pretended we were having huge knock-down, drag-out fights, without the knocking down and the dragging out. We'd tell juicy stories about well-known people in the neighborhood. And then, as the stock-market bubble was just forming, I started making it sound as if I had insider stock-trading information. I didn't, but we weren't under oath. Besides, **they** were eavesdropping on **us**! I'd mention how I was investing in Intel and "buying huge lots of Cisco," at a time when nobody had ever heard of it. "Why are they buying lots of Crisco?" they'd wonder. Do those people **fry** everything?

But our most dramatic performance started with a ringing doorbell, with my wife greeting the gentleman caller, me. Then there was some rustling and whatnot. Next came sounds that many associate with starting a family. Of course the missus and I were sitting at the kitchen table acting it out.

Then we added some dialog. I asked her if her husband had figured out what was going on between the two of us. He'd be heartbroken if he found that his wife was having an affair with his own brother who he'd tried to kill with his bare hands at sleepaway camp! And did her husband know that their baby...was actually his? It was so **Knots Landing**. (Note to Younger Readers Who Don't Remember **Knots Landing:** Watch the History Channel.)

We had positioned ourselves near a window, so we could see the apartments we were presumably broadcasting into. I told her I had to "get back to work," and that I'd be leaving by the front door. She said "Good-bye" with a big smooching sound she made by kissing her own hand. Married people don't kiss like that during the cold and flu season.

We had set the trap.

Just as I slammed the door, I jogged back to the window to watch the apartment building across the way. If anybody had heard our Emmyworthy performance, they'd surely want to see that cad who was sleeping with his brother's wife as he left the building. A quick jangle of venetian blinds on the third floor, and we had a winner. For the first time we saw Wilma Flintstone holding Baby Jessica. In that instant I saw that Wilma was a smoker. Poor Baby Jessica. At least down that well there'd been no secondhand smoke.

MRS. HAPPY'S ADVICE

Parents holed up for thousands of hours at home with crying babies deserve combat pay. If they can find a creative way to pass the time, terrific.

We did, with our little innocent fun. Besides, had the eavesdropping neighbors actually acted on my husband's

phony insider-trading information and bought Cisco at two dollars and Intel $1.60, they would now be multi-millionaires many times over. If they did, they're rich, and we've not.

So now who's the joke on?

NANNYGATE

Finding a Babysitter

My attendance at the Emmy Award ceremonies was required, and due to an Academy of Television Arts & Science rule that they not allow anyone shorter than Emmanuel Lewis through the door, we had to find somebody to care for our seven-month-old. It would be the first time that either his mother or I would not be within ten feet to wipe up any impromptu drool.

Because our blood kin were all more than two thousand miles away, we called a well-respected but very expensive nanny agency. I mention expensive because I was informed over the phone that in addition to the twenty-dollar-an-hour charge, there would also be a payment for travel time and a late-night surcharge. We were first-timers, and we'd have paid our baby's weight in Krugerrands just to make sure he was still breathing and hadn't been kidnapped by Colombian drug lords at the conclusion of the evening.

I was surprised when I opened the door and saw a cute twenty-ish brunette. I'd been expecting somebody who looked nannyish—not necessarily Mary Poppins, but at least Mrs. Doubtfire. And how about a uniform, or at least an exotic European accent? Instead we were entrusting our baby to this college coed, who we were certain would be drinking beer from a funnel as soon as we pulled out of the driveway.

"Have fun, I've got everything under control," she assured us as she closed the door. For the first time in his life, we were leaving our baby in the hands of a total stranger. We stopped ten feet from our front door. My wife was a nervous wreck.

"Don't worry, they're bonded!" I reminded her.

"What's bonded mean?" my wife asked. "If they lose him, we get our security deposit back?"

She had a point. They probably lose kids all the time, and just pay some fine, less the $250 deductible. That was not going to happen to us, so I walked over to the sitter's car and wrote down her license plate and VIN. This would be handy for the FBI when they launched the nationwide manhunt for our baby.

Three hours later we returned and found our son **in his crib asleep**. We were so thankful that the nanny hadn't pulled a Bruno Hauptmann, we tipped her forty dollars. In the end we wound up paying her on average a dollar a minute.

"Peace of mind" is why my wife said it was a good investment. At this rate, if we wanted to go out for a dinner and a show once a week, we would need to start making direct deposit into the nanny's account, so we launched a search for a new sitter.

The first candidate did have a British accent of some kind, and she also wore a nurse's uniform, but she wasn't really a nurse, she just played one. In reality, she should have been dressed in camouflage, because she was pure drill sergeant. It would not have shocked me to hear her bark at my toddler, "Assume the position and give me twenty" while we were gone. We hired her three times, just until she'd taught our son some basic platoon-marching drills, and then we scratched her from the list.

The next young lady was sent our way by an agency with an impressive name that sounded like it was a division of the federal government. They provided child care for diplomats and government officials. She seemed perfect. She was playful and fun, and my son loved it when she read him **Scuffy the Tugboat.** One rainy day in New York, she asked if she could borrow my umbrella. At fifteen bucks an hour, I wanted her off the clock as soon as possible. "I'll return it next time," she promised. And out into the rain she went.

"There won't be a next time," my wife ominously announced from the other room.

Two minutes earlier as I'd been paying the sitter, my wife had sat down on the living room couch only to discover a note wedged between two of the cushions. She didn't know what it was when she opened it, and she certainly had no intention of prying into the sitter's personal life, but the headline was so catchy, she had to read it: "I want to kill my brother." That just screams READ ME. This note was apparently an assignment from her psychiatrist, to write about her torment and feelings of being trapped. "When I kill myself I want to go out in a blaze of glory."

It was that closing line that made it clear we were in the market for a nonsuicidal babysitter who wouldn't torch the joint before we returned from Bloomingdale's.

It took a year before we found another person we completely trusted. Sitters are like gold—once you find a good one, you like to brag a little. A couple we were friendly with was also looking for a sitter and seemed a little jealous that we'd latched on to someone honest and trustworthy.

One Saturday night, when the sitter was presiding over our children, our neighbor friend knocked on our door and asked if we were home, even though she knew we were gone. When the sitter explained that we were out, our friend said, "Oh, don't bother. I'll talk to them in the morning."

Then, with one shot at hijacking our sitter, she struck. "I know they don't use you every weekend, but if you'd like full-time work, you could come work for us. I'll pay your dental." And **poof,** our sitter with the overbite was gone.

The moral to this story is, if you have a great sitter you want to keep, clam up, or somebody is going to steal her or him from under your nose. You may feel the sitter is loyal to you, but when given the choice between health benefits and your frozen pizza, which would **you** choose?

Finally, we were desperate, until on our grocery store's bulletin board, buried under photocopied ads for garage sales, missing cats, and miracle weight loss potions, my wife spotted WILL BABYSIT. She pulled off one of the twenty hanging chads with a phone number and called the advertiser for a personal interview.

The woman arrived in a Chevy van smoking a Lucky Strike. We watched her take one final drag on the cigarette and then grind the life out of it with her work boot in our driveway. She was stout and direct. She had a hearty laugh and a shockingly dirty mouth. During her sit-down with my wife, I wrote down her license-plate number and called a police friend who ran the tag. The car was not stolen.

That Friday we got our first test drive with her. We told her we'd be back in three hours. But two hours into the date, we ran out of steam, and decided to surprise her. When we returned, we found her in the kitchen, down on all fours.

"Ride me!" she shouted, balancing two kids on her back. All three froze when they saw us. It was honestly the first time we'd come home to hear anybody screaming "Ride me!" in the kitchen. My son was visibly disappointed.

"You're early!" he whined. "Can you leave so we can play some more?" We complied and went to the deck, turned on the bug zapper, and waited to run out the clock. With a flash of the porch light, we knew that it was safe to come in. We'd finally found a nonfelon, happy-go-lucky, child-friendly sitter. We used her for most of my son's Wonder Years, until that fateful day when she asked if we would recommend her for a job with a family that needed full-time help. This conflicted us. If we did the right thing and told them how fabulous she was, they'd hire her, and we'd wind up looking for somebody new, who would certainly light the curtains on fire before we returned from the Olive Garden. Or we could sandbag her and tell the prospective employer that we once saw her wearing a tinfoil hat, talking into the toaster, and then we'd be able to keep her forever.

We told the truth and they hired her. She was a terrific nanny and a great pony.

MRS. HAPPY'S ADVICE

Your first choice for babysitting should be a blood relative. They have a natu-

ral bond to the child, and they won't gouge you like a total stranger.

Total strangers are fine as long as they have good references, answer all of your questions, and are not currently on a terrorist watch list. If possible, first have them visit before you leave them alone with your child to gauge their reaction. If it goes well, hire her on the spot. If you need a hostage negotiator to separate the two, go back to the supermarket and pull another name off the bulletin board and repeat the interview process.

Finally, if you ever come home, reach for the door, and hear "Ride me!" pray that it's either something on television or your Sears riding mower has developed the ability to talk.

SAY WHAT?

Kids Say the Darnedest Things

My children know too much.

Because they are embedded at our home, they see it all. **Usually** they keep it to themselves.

"Daddy says you're a drunk," popped out of my son's mouth at a company picnic. He was taking to my ex-boss. I don't think my ex-boss remembered it later—I got lucky, he was plastered.

Children are at their most vulnerable to blab when they are between the ages of three and eight. That's a five-year window when you should have a piece of duct tape at the ready if Junior starts acting as if his juice box is full of sodium Pentothal.

During the ride home after the company-picnic faux pas we instructed our son that he was to never again repeat in public anything he heard at home. All of our catty comments and family secrets would remain our family secrets.

He was a man of his word. For two months.

It was bedtime and my son was watching my wife change his sister's diaper. He usually wasn't interested in her humdrum baby routine, but as is the case with children of that age, he'd do anything to not go to bed, so he was acting interested to run out the clock. He was right at eye level with the diaper-change zone and he got a Panavision view when his sister surprised both of them by soaking the changing table and the immediate vicinity. He'd never seen how a girl relieved bladder buildup from that vantage point, and it was at that moment that he realized for the first time that he and his sister were built differently in the plumbing department.

"I see her butt, but where's her penis, Mommy?"

He had recently transformed from adorable, perfect genius boy to an inquisitor with seventy-five questions an hour, expecting us to respond when he asked an embarrassing or awkward question. My wife read in a parenting book that you should answer those direct body-part questions with accurate information. So she used her Mother Goose voice to explain that "boys have penises and girls have vaginas."

The last part sounded a lot like where we lived and it just didn't add up, so he asked a follow-up. "I know we live in Virginia, but where's her penis?" She explained again, and he nodded, but she knew he didn't understand. So she changed the subject. "Who wants some Swedish Fish?" and the whole penis-vagina thing vaporized.

The next day, during the family grocery checkout at Safeway, Bob the Checker asked how everybody was doing.

"The little one has started teething," my wife started, and just on cue, the baby peeked out of her seat, chewing on a completely drool-covered hand and generally looking miserable.

As my wife was writing out the check, my son, who'd apparently felt a little neglected in the conversation, decided it was time for "all eyes on me" and piped up: "My sister has a penis in her butt."

Bob stopped scanning the groceries and gave my wife the same stink eye he reserved for people who tried to cash in an expired coupon.

"I saw it," my boy continued. "Last night. She had a penis in her butt."

All commerce stopped at that checkout aisle and the two adjacent. My wife had simply dropped in for something to barbecue and now had the same feeling you get when you realize your house is surrounded by a SWAT team from Social Services. Hey, lady, you with the London broil, come out with your hands up!

A speedy payment, a few shifty glances, and the trio made a hasty retreat to the parking lot. She understood how kids' minds work, reconstructing what her son had said, and knew that the sight of his sister peeing, with it running down her backside, combined with the fact that "boys have penises and girls have vaginas," added up to "My sister has a penis in her butt." She could explain it if she had to, but she didn't think she needed to explain it to a guy wearing a big button that said IT'S DOUBLE COUPON DAY! Just then she realized in a panic that she'd left some of her groceries at the checkout and had to return to the scene of the crime.

"Has anybody seen my meat?" They had, and Bob presented her with the package. She zipped back to the parking lot and opened the rear door of the Volvo station wagon. Slamming it down, she moved the kids and the cart to the side door and opened it, only to discover that the car seats had been stolen. Then she noticed the cigarette smoke in the car, and knowing she hadn't been gone long enough for someone to commit a double car-seat theft **and** smoke a cigarette, she realized it was not her Volvo station wagon. She looked around and there, one row over in the identical spot, was her vehicle. Child endangerment is one thing, but when you add grand theft auto, suddenly you're in Movie of the Week land.

No state employees ever showed up at our house. We switched supermarkets.

MRS. HAPPY'S ADVICE

Never say anything in front of your children that you don't want broadcast throughout your neighborhood. It's like the Miranda warning meets Desperate Housewives: anything you say can and will be used against you on your cul-de-sac.

PARENT TRAP

A Parent's Pop Quiz

This is a test of the Emergency Parenting System. These things really happened. If you were the PIC (parent in charge), what would you do?

QUESTION 1

Your child is having a playdate, and you notice your young visitor is foaming at the mouth, and it looks like rabies. What is the correct response?

A. Call 911.
B. Immediately administer CPR.
C. Blame it on the Easter Bunny.

My wife answered C.

My five-year-old daughter was playing with her kindergarten friend Lauren on the day Lauren's brother was having a very serious brain operation—the last thing her mother needed was to worry about Lauren, so my wife volunteered to take care of her.

It was Easter week, and the planned activity was dyeing eggs. The kitchen table was covered with newspapers, and the place was stinking of vinegar and boiling eggs. Feeling a little left out of the "big-girl fun," our three-year-old tried to get their attention by offering them Skittles. Dyeing eggs **and** getting tanked up on sugar. "My mom never lets me have candy after school," Lauren said.

The eggs were finally out of the pot and cool enough to color, so my wife was carrying them to the table when she noticed that Lauren was foaming at the mouth.

"SHE'S GOT RABIES!" is what was screaming in my wife's head. "Is everybody having fun?" is what came out of her mouth.

Of course they were. They were eating Skittles and dyeing hard-boiled eggs, which smelled gassy. "Lauren, is that you?" my daughter joked, which led to more giggles and gas jokes. "Maybe it's not rabies," my wife hoped, praying for just a simple seizure. "Great," she remembers thinking. "The family has one kid in the hospital, and I'm killing the other." Not a screamer, my wife grabbed the kitchen first-aid manual and looked for "red foaming mouth" as the three-year-old offered her a candy.

"Skittle, Mommy?"

"No thanks" just left her lips when she looked at the candy and realized it wasn't a Skittle her daughter was offering but a blue egg-dye tablet. That's what Lauren had chewed on! That meant she didn't have rabies—she'd been poisoned!

Three minutes later, a voice at the Poison Control hot line assured her the tablets were not dangerous.

"We get these calls all the time," the operator assured her.

"Not on my watch," my wife signed off.

Lauren's brother's operation was a success. Nobody would have found out about the rabies

thing had Lauren not gone home with a mouthful of red teeth, which made it look like she'd
spent the afternoon at our house drinking Bloody
Marys. Lauren was never left in our care again.
She would have to contract rabies somewhere
else.

QUESTION 2

The flower girl at the wedding is turning
blue. What should you do?

A. Call 911.
B. Immediately administer CPR.
C. Blame the groom.

We almost did A, then were about to commence
B, but in the end we just did C.

My sister had just tied the knot, and in those
always hectic few minutes after the vows, just
before the new couple walks out of the church
to a waiting car, the official wedding photograph
had to be taken. I was her designated shutterbug,
trying to get everybody to look in the same direction. My wife was simultaneously camcordering
the event.

"Pretend you like each other," I joked. They
giggled and grinned. **Snap, snap, snap**.

Behind me I noticed a tiny cough. I turned to
see the three-year-old flower girl, my daughter.

She appeared to be smiling, but as a parent you have a catalog of every sound in your child's repertoire, and this cough was odd. A second later there was another. This was yet a different cough. It wasn't a cough, she was choking!

"Did you eat a flower?" seemed like the logical question you'd ask the flower girl. She shook her head. "Is it candy?" Another head shake. Her complexion started turning icy blue. We'd recently completed a baby CPR class, and we knew what to do.

"ABC!" I told my wife, then announced out loud that ABC meant Airway, Breathing, Circulation.

"Airway: Is there something blocking her throat?"

"Give her a glass of water," someone suggested.

"Can you Heimlich a kid?" someone blurted out. More coughs; she was now much bluer, then tears came. For somebody choking to death, she was remarkably calm. As we stood there asking questions, she started a series of gut-wrenching dry coughs, until just like a cat belting out a fur ball, she sent a projectile two feet straight out of her mouth. It wasn't a flower. It wasn't a candy. It was a quarter.

If we had given her a glass of water as someone suggested, that could have lodged it more firmly in her throat. Given that we were in a church, a member of the family suggested it was the hand of God that saved her, and a round of "Amen"s followed.

We were terrified, but apparently so was the flower girl, because the rest of the day, whenever somebody would ask her how she was, she replied with the same canned statement of fact: "Don't eat da money."

Of course I blame the groom, because it happened at **his** church, where apparently they don't sweep the aisles for cash as they do at my church, Our Lady of the Perpetual Fund-Raiser.

The next day my father inquired as to how she was doing. She repeated her new mantra: "Don't eat da money."

My father told her, "That's right, don't eat the money." Then he showed the grace and compassion he's famous for. "Grandpa needs a newspaper. Can you cough up another quarter?"

MRS. HAPPY'S ADVICE

Know everything you can about first aid. When in doubt, call the doctor. Or 911. Don't waste time.

Take a CPR class.

Buy only predyed Easter eggs.

If anything bad happens at a wedding, do what most brides do, and just blame the groom.

MAKING THE GRADE

Time for School

Small children are cute for only so long, and at some point they'll start to annoy you and you'll want them to leave for a few hours during the day. While they're too young for the army or to enter the manager-trainee program at Mail Boxes Etc., there is a place they can go when they're of age: school.

The first day of school is, without fail, a trauma for Momma. My wife went wobbly when she discovered public education's dirty little secret. "They don't have seat belts on the bus!"

Our child shouldn't even have been on the bus. His school was only a quarter mile from our house, and yet a kooky state law mandated that all children were to be transported to and fro in a large, bright yellow state-owned vehicle not equipped with seat belts.

"I'm tailing 'em!" my wife announced to the next-door neighbor as she climbed into her SUV. The neighbor, who also was sending her child off for the first day, hopped in and rode shotgun. They were both terrified of what was waiting for the driver at the end of our street. The driver would have to make a left turn across four lanes of open highway, and my wife wanted to be there "just in case." An out-of-control eighteen-wheeler never barreled toward the kids, and my wife's escort did nothing but satisfy her normal parental paranoia.

Most children eagerly anticipate school; they love the idea of new friends, new activities, and new challenges.

"The day is too long," my son complained after his first day.

Our middle child shook hands with each person she encountered on day one. "Nice to meet you," she said again and again. I had to admire her ability to speak to total strangers. One day she'll be either president or the greeter at Wal-Mart.

My wife was visiting a potential preschool for our three-year-old when a tough girl named Brittany walked over, ripped my daughter's glasses off, and threw them into a box of Brio blocks. Then she pulled her hair, drew a stick hangman on her forearm, and finished my daughter off with a bite on the throat.

"Brittany, say you're sorry," instructed the principal, who'd been giving the tour.

The evil preschooler just stood there glaring at my daughter. My wife stood there stunned at the child's insolence, and then the principal got stupid. "Well, it's Brittany's choice to apologize or not, and apparently she's chosen not."

My wife then chose not to enroll our pumpkin in a school where the adults kowtow to pint-sized terrorists and discipline is a nice idea but is rarely enforced—apparently it would have been bad for business in a school of future Tonya Hardings.

Because children spend so many hours with their teachers, they frequently fall in love with them, although their parents sometimes aren't crazy about what they're teaching. In first grade my son's teacher had a counting chart on the wall that was a tote board of the number of baby teeth each kid would lose over the course of the year. It was a race to see who'd be the class jack-o'-lantern. During a routine parent-teacher conference my wife pointed out that the baby-tooth chart was driving my son nuts, because he was the only kid in the class who still had his complete first batch of God-given teeth. "Relax," the teacher said, "he'll just have to get used to it." How could he get used to being in last place **every day**? He didn't lose a tooth that year, or the next or the next. It wasn't until fifth grade that one of his teeth finally popped out. The tooth fairy brought him a twenty. Nothing erases childhood trauma like a substantial cash settlement.

Preschool is also where many children experience their first taste of romance. My wife found this note in our big girl's backpack: "Marry me, and I will buy you a Barbie doll."

Once again an exchange of property turns heads, especially a second-grader's when it's a Mattel product hanging in the balance. This was a particularly touching offer, because the boy's own mother's name was Barbie. This real-life Barbie mom got a great deal of attention from the dads in the class, as she was a very attractive blonde who frequently wore leopard-print clam diggers and gold high heels. By the way, our daughter never collected on the doll dowry, as we have a family rule that nobody gets married until they're old enough to get a Blockbuster card.

The grade-school years are so special. This is when children learn the skills they'll need to one day get a job or commit wire fraud. So many people say, "Enjoy this time, it goes by so fast," and it really does. In no time our firstborn was in high school. I still remember the parents' orientation in the school cafeteria.

"Look around," the hired speaker announced. "Half of your kids are gay! Get used to it." Parents sat slack-jawed as the speaker told a tale of woe that essentially went like this: "You think you know your child, but unless you crack down now, one day when you're not watching, your son or daughter will become a sketchy character who'd steal the family car, print a fake ID with Windows XP, buy toxic alcoholic beverages, and then crash the car into that oak tree in front of your house and die. Any questions?"

"And there's a fifty-fifty chance your child is GAY!" he barked at the stunned crowd. The only motivation this "motivational speaker" provided was to send your child to private school. The people who really needed to hear his message, the incoming freshman class, had not attended the scare-a-thon. They were at a mixer. My son's first. We don't know what happened there that night, but whatever it was, it was not a good thing. My son didn't go to another high school dance for three years.

At some point during your children's school days they will come home and ask if it's okay if they join the band, or go out for the team, but if they ever ask, "Is it okay if I run for class office?" be forewarned. Each of my children has done this. They all ran clean campaigns, on platforms with lofty goals—organizing charity events for the community's less fortunate and adding more social events for the school's socially-minded. Meanwhile, their opponents were outright liars, who made campaign promises like "If you vote for me, I'll get J. K. Rowling to come to our school and read the new Harry Potter book!" That person won by a landslide. So did the kid who simply promised, "No homework, and free candy ALL DAY LONG!"

All the way from elementary through high school my son ran for class offices. Each year there seemed to be some sort of scandal. Forget Florida's hanging chads; that was a third-rate bookkeeping error compared with the rumors of electioneering and worse we heard year after year from members of the school board. Where are those United Nations monitors when you need them? After one disturbing dispatch from the cafeteria, a call of concern was made to the principal, who announced at the end of the day that the results were in and for the first time in the school's history, it was a tie. The next day, after a night of phone banking and retail campaigning, another election was held, and my son won, so we never questioned the outcome.

Meanwhile, my daughter couldn't compete with the absolute liars who promised that Wayne Gretzky would come to school as Principal for a Day. She instead vowed that if she were elected, her class would take part in more charity events and have more fun. Charity doesn't get votes. What got her elected was this pledge: "If elected, I promise to replace the sandpaper-like toilet paper with quality quilted four-ply." She won in a landslide. To make good on the campaign promise, my wife bought three cases of Charmin at Kmart.

Why are school elections so dirty? Because all kids' parents dream of having that extra line on their offspring's college application saying that they were **senior class president**. They reason that if a kid doesn't win that office, he won't get into his dream college, which means he won't get a job offer from the premier employer in his field, which means he won't join the town's most exclusive country club where his wife will be hit on by the club pro. In other words, if a kid doesn't promise "Lindsay Lohan will teach home ec," she won't win and her life will effectively be over, even before it gets started, and they might as well spend their time trying to pick up girls by promising Barbie dolls.

At the end of the school road waits graduation. As soon as the high school band started playing "Pomp and Circumstance" at our oldest's graduation, I heard what I thought was a reaction to seasonal allergies: sniffling. It was my missus; I turned to see tears streaming down her face. "My job is done," she whispered.

She was right. As parents we do our best to fill the heads of those kids in mortarboards with facts and figures and the knowledge of what's right and what's wrong. Then it's up to them. But my wife didn't need to hear me agree.

"It's never done," I said. "Today we tell him to pick up his clothes and floss his teeth, but in thirty years we'll still be bossing him around: 'Put more in your IRA and diversify your portfolio.'"

But she wasn't buying it, and suddenly I got a little wobbly. In ninety days he would start as a freshman at a college that would cost $42,500 a year. Multiply that by four years, and triple the total when his sisters follow. That meant the midlife-crisis car I'd been planning since before I got married, would probably have to wait another ten. By then I'd have a ridiculous comb-over and the last thing I'd need would be a red convertible.

I dreamed of a soft top in my future; instead I see a latex glove and a prostate exam.

MY BOY IN THE BUBBLE

Are You Too Protective?

Two days before my son's eighteenth birthday, I did what most parents never do. I actually looked at the eight-millimeter—all seventy-three of them—videotapes I'd dutifully created with my Sony camcorder at every birthday and school recital of his life. I looked at summer vacations and the occasional dog washing.

Three observations:

1. I should have turned on that antijiggle feature.
2. We spent a fortune on birthday ponies.
3. Perhaps we'd raised "the boy in the bubble" without an actual plastic bubble.

Did we go overboard in the protection department?

It was one of those things that you don't realize you're doing when you're doing it, but when you have the benefit of time and distance, it's easy to see some things. We took our jobs seriously and had insulated him from all dangers, real and imagined, and now that he was on the verge of manhood, we wondered which of these things we'd done he would mention first to the shrink he'd start seeing when he's thirty to figure out "why my parents messed me up."

Let's examine the evidence.

Toys

As I watched eighteen Christmas mornings back-to-back, I realized that despite the fact that we wanted him to grow up to be a normal boy, we never gave him what he really wanted: a gun. Not a real gun, but a toy Uzi or automatic pistol or something that he could aim at squirrels and neighbor kids and squeeze off a round from when he felt the urge.

He didn't get one because we'd read a few of those "How to Be the Perfect Parent" articles and they made it clear that guns glorified warfare and violence. If kids played with toy guns, the research indicated, they would wind up oblivious to the difference between good and evil, and one day we'd get a call from a college dean to inform us that our son was up in the bell tower blasting away at coeds.

So he never got a gun. Later we discovered the urge to shoot things is programmed into boys at the factory, and by the time he was three he was shooting at squirrels in the trees and rabbits in the yard with his fingers locked in a pistol-like pose; later he improvised a weapon from a bent stick and shot at the Good Humor truck.

On his eighteenth birthday, to make up for his ammo-free childhood, I toyed with the idea of giving him a set of brass knuckles and napalm, but my black-market sources had dried up, and he had to settle for luggage.

Water Hazards

Like the Beverly Hillbillies, we had a "cement pond" in our backyard. At first we thought it was so handy having a 52,000-gallon swimming pool just ten feet from the house, but shortly after our boy started walking, we stopped sleeping because we were positive that in the night he would slip out the back door and go swimming straight to the bottom. So to make sure he didn't go into the pool without us, we locked every door. We had a pool cover and a state-of-the-art floating alarm that would in theory shriek when something fell into the water. In reality if the wind blew more than five miles an hour, it would make a wave in the pool and the alarm would wake up the neighbors.

When we did use the pool, he always wore something inflatable. And I'm not talking about those little blow-up things that go on the arms. We outfitted him in a coast guard–approved full-body floatation device. There he was on the videotape from his third birthday, encased in this blaze-orange inner tube that stretched from his shoulders to his crotch. It had taken two people fifteen minutes to install him in it, so when it was time to ride the pony, we decided it wasn't worth the trouble of taking it off, so he rode the horse while inside the floatation device. He looked like a bloated cowboy. If Leonardo DiCaprio had had one of these, his character would have been available for **Titanic II**.

Scary Foods

You've heard that the trans fats in French fries can kill people, but did you know that something even more diabolical is probably lurking in your kitchen right now?

We'd taken a child CPR class shortly before our son was born. The instructors made it clear that the most dangerous thing in your house is not a loaded gun; it's a grape. Grapes are just the size of a kid's windpipe, and if they eat a bunch of them quickly, one might get stuck and cut off the air supply. They said hot dogs were also exactly the diameter of a kid's throat and great caution must be used when consuming Oscar Mayers. They were both fine to eat, we were told, as long as they were cut up. From that day forward, whenever we had grapes, or an unknown-meat-filled-frank, we'd always cut them into molecule-sized bites.

On my son's first day of preschool, my vigilant wife asked the teacher what the morning snack would be.

Grapes, she was told. "Will they be cut in half?" she asked.

When the principal stopped laughing, she said no, and my wife promptly volunteered to work in the kitchen herself and personally halved fifteen pounds of green grapes.

That was the last time she ever asked what was on the menu.

MRS. HAPPY'S ADVICE

How has the human race survived over tens of thousands of years with all of these scary things on the planet? Crocodiles, volcanoes, and grapes! "Look, he's got a whole weiner next to the swimming pool! Call a SWAT team!"

When I was a child my mother let me have a toy gun and ride my bike throughout the neighborhood, unsupervised, without a helmet; we even sometimes went swimming less than an hour after a full meal. And somehow I turned out okay. We did have rules; I was not allowed to speak to strangers, play in abandoned refrigerators, or hang out with that neighbor boy who

tortured cats with a magnifying glass on sunny days.

Whatever you let your kids do, be wise and supervise.

Looking over the videotape evidence, I realized we probably did overdo it on our firstborn, but we quickly adjusted. Now we watch new parents and admire how they're overdoing it.

"The Kryptonite stroller, that's a nice touch," I say to Mr. Happy.

WHERE DID WE GO WRONG?

Worst-Case Scenarios

Sometimes our little angels seem to be Satan's handmaidens. Like the time

- A high school teenager, short on cash for beer, got a suggestion from his friends: "Sell your mom's car." Under the influence of idiots, he thought it was a great idea. A phone call was made, and soon he dropped off the car on an unfamiliar New York corner. He netted $250 cash for his mom's new Lexus. He was told he was grounded until his AARP membership packet arrives.

- A seventh-grade girl invited her entire class to an unsupervised party while her parents were out of town. The house got trashed. She was worried that her parents would hit the roof. When Mom returned, she saw the devastation and was delighted. If seventy-five kids showed up, that meant "my daughter is popular!"
- A sixteen-year-old girl invited forty-five classmates to her house while her parents were on vacation. The minors emptied a liquor cabinet, and one guest stole five hundred dollars cash from the family's emergency drawer. The burglar left three hundred behind, thinking nobody would notice five C-notes missing. When the folks got home, the girl got grounded one week for each hundred dollars missing.
- Upon returning from a business trip, a high school boy's parents heard a heart-wrenching story: "Mom, Dad, when I was sleeping, vandals came into the house and wrecked it!" That's how he explained the holes in the walls, the dining room light that had been pulled out of the ceiling, and how the family dog had been "probed." The parents overlooked the seventy-eight empty beer bottles in the recycling bin and a copy of a police report filed after the neighbors called to com-

plain. The insurance company didn't buy the vandalism thing, and the parents paid to patch the house and perpetuate the myth themselves.

CRIME AND PUNISHMENT

Discipline

My wife knows something about discipline. As a child growing up in Los Angeles, she was pitching a fit in a grocery-store checkout line, demanding a Hershey bar. "I told you no!" her mother firmly stated.

"But I **waaaaaaannnt** it!" she wailed.

It went back and forth like that for about a minute, until they heard a slow and measured voice from behind them in the line: "Give the little lady the candy, ma'am." They turned to see fellow Encino resident John Wayne, the biggest star in Hollywood, nod in their direction and then mouth "Now."

My wife got the candy and her mother got a wink from the Duke. Sadly, John Wayne is no longer settling domestic-disturbance cases at grocery stores, but my wife has developed a keen sense of what it takes to bring civility to a family.

"Be a family," she says when talking about disciplining children. "As in organized-crime family."

She doesn't mean a kid who's been naughty should wake up with a horse head in bed. There simply aren't enough horse heads to go around. But she makes a good argument that families should consider adopting a few crime-family tricks. Bribes, strong-arm tactics, lip service, and a modified witness-relocation program.

Strong-Arm Tactics

There is an impulse when your kid is doing something **really** bad to spank him. I have felt it, and it doesn't take Dr. Joyce Brothers to know that it's probably because I was spanked as a juvenile offender. I still remember the day, forty-some years ago, I had the misfortune of waiting until the exact moment my mother was walking into the dining room to use a dirty word out loud for the first time in my life to describe a surprise the family dog left on the floor.

"Where did you hear that?" she demanded.

"Daddy." It was true. As you know, the truth is not always a good defense. So I wound up going upstairs with Mommy so she could wash my mouth out with soap.

She scraped a new bar of Ivory back and forth on my teeth. The result was not only a dazzling white smile, but the spaces between my teeth were now filled in with whiteness; I had movie-star Chiclet teeth. That was good. The bad part was that over the next two weeks, at random times, a piece of soap debris would dislodge and hit the taste sensors of my tongue, sending an electrical reminder through my system that I'd been a bad boy. That punishment worked. I learned my lesson and never again said that word…in front of my mother.

I spent many a moment on the receiving end of a red-hot hand. The key to enduring a spanking, I'd been told, was not to let them see you cry. That would mean they'd won, and you'd lost control. What a crock. Any time you get your bottom warmed up, you're a certified loser. I clearly remember thinking once, when freshly spanked, "I hate my parents!" And who wouldn't? Moments earlier I had been watching **Lost in Space**; then Dad got home and Mom sequestered him in the kitchen to inform him of whatever that day's infraction was. I got a modified version of the birthday paddling (one whack for each year), but this spanking was on steroids.

So what does spanking really accomplish? It makes the **parents** feel like they've done something. As a parent, I'm not a spanker. Okay, once there was some spankage. Our firstborn boy, at around the age of two, ran into the street and just narrowly missed getting run over by one of our friendly neighbors in that boat of a Buick they drove. Naturally I was on the verge of an exploding embolism; I grabbed him, flipped him like a flapjack over my knee, and gave him one firm swat. "You can't go in the street!" I screamed in my father's voice.

He never went back into the street.

Witness-Relocation Program

When mobsters sing like canaries, the government can send them to a new location. Kids hate new locations, they like their current locations; that's why the time-out is so effective. If our children behaved badly in front of visitors, I'd take them aside, tell them what an embarrassing act they'd just committed, and then relocate them to the penalty box, their room. "No, please!" they'd wail, "I'll be good!" They didn't want to miss any of the action downstairs, however, they had to learn their lesson. Once imprisoned, I'd set the kitchen timer on the microwave. Fifteen minutes covered most infractions, unless there'd been skin breakage, and then the timer would be replaced by a calendar.

Bribes

Occasionally the only way to accomplish something is with hush money.

If you're flying somewhere with a child, just say up front, "If you are a good boy/girl during this flight, I'm going to make sure we (fill in the blank with something they like) when we get there."

To make the bribe effective, show the kids the payoff. Hold up the Gummi Bears. Welcome to the Wonderful World of Blackmail.

Halfway through the flight, maybe you dole out half of the booty. Then at the end of the trip the ransom is delivered in full. Beware: If you promise a Mr. Misty float in exchange for their cooperation, and they fulfill their end of the bargain and no Mr. Misty materializes, you've just lost your street cred. Why should they ever believe you again? You'd better deliver, like Domino's.

P.S.: Only the parent can initiate a deal. If a road trip is looming and your kid says, "I'll be real good the whole way for fifty dollars," you've officially raised a grifter. Call Juvenile Hall and book him a bed. On the other hand, those are the kinds of negotiation skills that make Fortune 500 CEOs millions of dollars.

Just know that if your kid asks for a fifty today, next time it'll be a hundred, and in a year he'll want a Saab.

Lip Service

Never allow kids to negotiate their way out of a punishment. Make it clear that you're the warden. And unless they can get the governor to call on their behalf, commuting their sentence, they'd better "take the recycling to the curb."

MRS. HAPPY'S ADVICE

The absolute key to our organized-crime family discipline regime is consistency. Once we lay down the law on something, there's no budging.

When our son was four, we were out to eat with our next-door neighbors at the Black-eyed Pea. (Try the Chicken Fried Chicken—it's delicious.) My boy was all wound up, being around his best friend and his brother and sucking down his third Coke. He did something that really bugged us. We gave him a stern look. He did it again. We gave him a warning. He did it again.

Game over. My husband apologized to our neighbors and carted our kid off to a waiting SUV for a quick trip home. He never disrupted a meal out again. I should point out that my husband left me with the neighbors at the table, and even though there were four of them, and just me, I felt obligated to apologize in some way for my child's outburst, and I wound up picking up the entire tab, which would have been fine, but they'd ordered three rounds of cocktails and appetizers and entrées and dessert and after-dinner drinks

and coffee. It was a gigantic bill. But I didn't complain. Instead I planted a long black hair in the kid's ice cream sundae to try to get a free meal, but the kid ate it.

I do not suggest planting a hair or even a dead bug in a meal to get something free. I've found that faking a heart attack works much better.

THE BIRDS, THE BEES, THE CARROT

Talking About Sex

The moaning man, bent over in acute pain, was briskly wheeled into the emergency room of a Los Angeles hospital. Trying to comfort him was my wife, who was a candy striper at the totally unqualified age of twelve. She and her twelve-year-old best friend, Ann, were in one of the ER examining rooms assisting the medical staff and offering comfort to the patients. Of course the only comfort she could offer by law was the latest copy of **Life** magazine. The patient was impatient, and he passed.

"How about **McCall's**?"

"No."

"Sir, I have the new **Popular Mechanics**?"

"Can somebody get this kid out of here!" he begged as a nurse entered the room. Wearing sensible shoes that only look good on a nurse, she was doing the preliminary work for the doctor, who would be in shortly. After she got past the perfunctory age, height, weight, and allergies questions, she finally asked, "What seems to be the problem?"

Twenty-nine years in this department, and she had never heard this one: "I've got a carrot in my butt." And with that she instructed the candy stripers to leave the examining room **stat**!

Puzzled about how such an odd thing could happen, the preteens talked between themselves until it was time to leave. Luckily for them, the president of the hospital, who just so happened to be Ann's father, was driving them home. Utilizing quasi-medical jargon as only a twelve-year-old aspiring nurse would, they asked the obvious.

"Why did that man have a carrot in his rectum, Dr. Wilson?"

Dr. Wilson was a man of great wisdom and candor. If anyone would know, it was he. "Apparently the man was in his garden. Naked. Somehow he tripped and fell on the carrot." Of course! Naked gardening. That made sense to my wife until twenty years later she read in some non-child publication a more realistic (and horrifying) explanation for the pain of the nude gardener.

Dr. Wilson dealt with the tricky question of a sexual situation the same way millions of parents do. He made up a story that seemed realistic to a child, because the truth would have scared gray hairs onto their little heads.

Thirty years later, my wife and I are now adults, and thanks to an always turned on television (so the family can see Daddy at work in the morning), the entire Monica Lewinsky case was digested over breakfast at our house.

"Mommy, what's oral sex?" inquired our nine-year-old.

And with that the grown-up former candy striper followed in the footsteps of the good doctor. She paused for a moment, considered the consequences, and responded, "Good question. Oral sex is when you **talk** about sex. You know, **oral** means 'talk.'"

"Thanks, Mom." Later that day our son probably confessed to the other grade-schoolers, "My poor mom, she doesn't know what oral sex is."

When my sixteen-year-old son was to spend the summer in England, my wife demanded that I have **the talk** with him. He and I were seated in section 52 of Yankee Stadium when I started the conversation I'd dreaded since the doctor told us, "It's a boy!"

"Now, son, while you're away, we won't be there to help you figure out what to do...what's wrong and what's right..."

Like a trapped animal, he immediately sensed that he was about to get "the sex talk," and he interrupted. "I know what you're getting at, and we don't have to talk about this now—"

"Mommy wants—"

"I heard about it in health class, okay?"

Wait a minute. I'd woken up at three that morning sweaty and nauseous because I was going to have to have a little talk with him, and he **already knew**! Fine with me. I knew that the football coach was the point person for his high school on the official Board of Education sex talk, and from what other parents had reported to us, it was graphic and left little to the imagination.

"Well, do you have any questions for **me** about it?" I asked, not really wanting to answer anything.

"No."

"Okay, good. I'm glad we had this talk."

Four years later it was my daughter's turn. She was just the opposite. While my boy didn't want to even touch his toe to the third rail, my daughter had many questions. After each health class, she'd pepper my wife with dozens of questions about birth control, family planning, and other uncomfortable female issues such as organ function and maintenance. Then, rather than speaking generally, she personalized. "Mommy, what birth control do you use, or are you in menopause?"

This was it. It was finally time to honestly answer a sex question. "I'm not menopausal," my wife said, "despite the volume at which I'm speaking."

My daughter took note. My wife continued. "**If** it ever happens to me, I'll let you know. And one more thing," she added. "Empty the dishwasher."

MRS. HAPPY'S ADVICE

When it comes time to talk to your offspring about sex, you should be honest and direct. Use age-appropriate jargon. If they are television watchers, you will probably be surprised at how much they already know.

There is no hurry to sit a six-year-old down and tell her that your earlier story about the stork was a lie. Storks don't deliver babies—they're in the pickle industry.

In the end they will find the information enlightening despite the nervous presentation by their parent. If you simply are not able to bring up the subject with your child, there are books that spell it all out. If you're uncomfortable with all of the above suggestions, you can always recite the story of the birds and the bees and the carrots.

DINE AND DASH

Feeding Time

Long ago, in that time known as B.C. (before children), husbands and wives ate quietly in their caves whatever food was plentiful. Yak Helper was huge. As their families expanded it was quickly discovered that their children didn't like man-sized portions of Yak Helper; they much preferred Yak Fingers or Yak 'n' Cheese.

Those lessons from early man still hold true today as families sit down to tie on the feed bag. Actually, a feed bag would be a good idea, because food-in-a-bag cleanup would not require a 1,250-psi high-pressure deck washer.

Extremely hungry kids will eat the grime off a mouse ball, but American kids are never really hungry because nine minutes before dinner they're hiding in the hall closet eating a yard of Froot by the Foot.

With our first child, my wife had digested the very latest food data from a series of hardbound child-rearing manuals. This material was generally written by constipated people who didn't have their own children. The consensus was that responsible parents should only feed their tiny diners "age-appropriate foods."

Okay, if that's what the book says, our son would get no sweets, no pizza, no fun. He didn't get the first taste of a French fry until he was eighteen months old. Please don't call the authorities; we've since revised our early-childhood menus. In fact, after our last child was born, we stopped on the way home from the hospital to pick up her first Happy Meal.

"Mmmmmmm, McFlurry..."

Don't ever make the mistake of asking a child what he wants. We once found ourselves the guests of my brother-in-law at a very expensive restaurant carved into the side of a Colorado mountain. Despite the fact that it was a family resort, there were no kid items on the menu. Our daughter would have to improvise off the big-people menu. We were delighted that she ordered butternut squash gnocchi.

"What an evolved palate," our otherwise surly waiter remarked. But that was before the meal arrived and our daughter got a good look at that plate of orange stuff. That started the standoff. "At least try a bite," we begged as we finished our entrées and she was foraging bread sticks from adjacent tables.

Parents are suckers when it comes to pleasing their children, and many ask what they want and then try to deliver. For instance, our middle child went through a stage where she would wear only pink clothes and eat only pink foods. Her choices were frighteningly few. Spaghetti with pink sauce and grapefruit. That was at the same time that she refused to poop, because "it's not beautiful."

The son of a very dear friend would occasionally come to eat at our house. And luckily, just like my kids, he loved pizza. Let me amend that—he loved pizza as long as it wasn't wearing any meat, vegetables, or red sauce. In other words, he ate only the crust. That's a cracker. My wife knew that, and when he arrived for dinner, she baked one up special just for him. He didn't touch it. His mother always baked a rectangular naked pizza, and my wife had built a round one.

She should have offered butternut squash gnocchi.

A playmate of our youngest stayed over for lunch one day. My wife knows how important choices are to children, so she carefully made three different kinds of sandwiches: peanut butter, cheese, and a "just bread" sandwich. She'd covered all of her sandwich bases. "Do you have macaroni and cheese?" the child inquired.

"I can make some with real cheese," my wife offered.

"Okay, I'll wait."

Out came the Disney cookbook, and twenty-two minutes later, a lovely three-cheese mac and cheese. "I'm sorry, but I only eat the Kraft kind," declared the pint-sized Emeril Lagasse. Steamed, my wife spun the lazy Susan and located the familiar blue box, and fourteen minutes later the critic had a spoonful of yellow glop. My wife was delighted to take the young guest home as quickly as possible and was surprised to hear on the drive, "Not to be rude, but I did not have a good time at your house."

Out to Eat

Because mealtime is so routine, it's always a great adventure for young diners to escape the family home and eat out. Restaurants love to see us because we are the first ones at the door. If it opens at five, we're the only early birds under seventy. Plus, the earlier we eat, the earlier relaxing beverages can be consumed without raising concern from the children. "Will you be having your medicine drink, Daddy?"

Aside from the variety of foods that will scare them, I have found that being in a family restaurant allows the children a freedom that they don't get at home, the ability to say, "I've got to use the bathroom" and then proceed to the potty two or three times, pre-entrée, just to luxuriate. You may be horrified by the lack of general hygiene, but they don't understand germs and they'll immediately drop trou and sit down on the bowl. Can I get you the sports page, Tiffany?

We have ventured out to area restaurants twice a week for the last eighteen years. And of all of those 1,872 restaurant visits, one stands out above all others.

It was 5:01 P.M.; we'd already been seated by a snooty guy in a tuxedo shirt at a delightful table located handily next to the kitchen. I'd just buckled our toddler into the high chair, after a hasty diaper change in the parking lot. A lovely older couple stopped by our table to poke their fingers in the baby's face, and using that high-pitched voice grown-ups use when in the general proximity of people sixty years their junior, the gentleman inexplicably said, "It's Miller time, get that kid a kamikaze!" The baby responded with the biggest grin you've ever seen. A smile so broad, eyes so squinty, face so red—the elders thought it was so cute, but that was no smile, our baby was pooping right before their very eyes.

At that moment Mr. Friendly in the tuxedo shirt asked them to reseat themselves and brought their dinner to their table. What transpired in the next two minutes was the most terrifying thing I've seen in a restaurant since that Mafia crime-family boss was gunned down outside of Sparks Steak House.

We knew that unless we immediately changed her diaper, our other two children would announce in loud voices, "Something's stinky!" So I volunteered to make a return trip to the parking lot. I threw the diaper bag over my shoulder, unbuckled her high-chair seat belt, and was just starting to lift her up when my middle child said in her outdoor voice, "Daddy, she's pooping on you!"

Ten minutes earlier, in my haste to get into the restaurant and have my first vodka and water on the rocks (hold the water, hold the rocks), I did not put that stupid pair of frilly pants on over her diaper. I'd always thought it was just for decoration. Today I was learning the hard way that they also can keep diapers in one place. They had come apart because I hadn't stuck the Pampers tapes in the right places, and now one entire side had fallen off. The result was that her bare butt was plopped directly on the high-chair seat.

At this moment what seemed like a six-week supply of "number two" had been hydraulically smashed into her high chair and on my new sage-brush Dockers.

The other two kids were now laughing as loud as they could because this was by far the funniest thing they'd ever seen in their lives, aside from the time they heard our neighbor have gas at the public library. It was at exactly that moment that our order materialized at the nearby kitchen door. Not wanting to freak out the waiter, I did the only humane thing: I plopped her back down into that pile of woe.

The waiter was oblivious to it all; he had no idea what diabolical subterfuge was in play at table 9. As he turned to leave, I handed the baby to my wife, who covered her bottom with a baby blanket and then dashed to the car. She left two baby wipes for me to clean up the devastation on the chair. I didn't need two, I needed two hundred. The chair had a rough particleboard finish (which I'm sure felt great on her bottom), and it was embedded with a lifetime supply of DNA. I sent one of the gigglers into the restroom, and he returned with one damp paper towel. I instructed the older kids to sit down and try to not look like anything had happened. I made a trip into the men's room and found a roll of Bounty towels. Maybe this happened all the time.

I scrubbed away for three minutes until my wife reappeared with the bundle of joy. By now the chair was clean enough, and she was redeposited (so to speak) there. My wife made sure that the baby was now wearing that frilly pair of diaper panties, which I am now a true believer in. In fact, I'm wearing some right now myself.

MRS. HAPPY'S ADVICE

When dining out, keep in mind the waiter's tip is based not on the service, but on the pile of food under your table. If your child threw 25 percent of his entrée on the floor, the tip is 25 percent. If 50 percent is on the floor, the tip is 50 percent. If the floor has received 75 percent of the food, the tip

is 15 percent, because you'll never be allowed back, so why bother sucking up to the waiter?

FREQUENT-CRIER MILES

Traveling with Kids

"I have some bad news and some worse news," the husband told the minivan passengers as they pulled out of the petrol station somewhere in rural France. "I just paid over a hundred euros to fill up the tank," he started.

"What's the worse news?" his wife asked.

"I just filled us up with unleaded. The pump was all in French. I meant to use diesel." And yet, despite his worry, the vehicle was running fine. For three hundred yards. Then it conked out. As the eight kids filed out, one of them branded him with a moniker that has stuck to him like stink on Camembert cheese.

"Good job, Diesel."

Traveling is hard. Traveling with children is harder.

Airline flight was once upon a time so special that male travelers wore jackets and ties. Now you're better off wearing a lobster bib, since the passenger next to you might well be a five-year-old gumming Laffy Taffy.

My children have been known to give some fellow travelers trouble. For instance, I remember the short flight on a Buddy Holly plane from Los Angeles to San Diego, when our little one kept pulling the hair of the passenger seated in front of her. It was actor Hal Holbrook, en route to one of his famous one-man shows as Abe Lincoln. I imagine the flight gave him plenty of new material. "Four score and seven neutered kids ago..."

Then there were our family trips to the tropics. In Jamaica, a man who I don't believe was working with the Drug Enforcement Agency came up to the kids and me and tried to sell us a brick of marijuana.

"No thanks, we're set. I've got a week's supply of Benadryl," I joked. After he tried to buy that from me, he asked if one of the kids could be a drug mule on the flight back. Despite my first inclination to always be helpful, we briskly walked away. My infant daughter, Sally, heard the word **mule** and blurted out "Mooooo!"

We jumped onto the bus that would wind through the back roads of Jamaica to our all-inclusive family resort. On the picturesque sales brochure they didn't mention that the resort was two and a half hours from the airport. Nor did they mention that the only scheduled stop during the trip would be at a roadside shack, where the operator gave our driver a Red Stripe beer, followed by another. I had been worried that he was stoned; now I had to worry that he was stoned **and** drunk.

Glancing around, I noticed that behind the counter, in the kitchen, where the guy was grilling jerk chicken, stood a goat. It wasn't there to make goat cheese; it was busy eating out of the refrigerator. When my daughter saw it, she said, "Mooooo."

My parents didn't take us on many trips growing up. Money was tight, but then again there was also the problem of what happened when we all got together.

On a cloudless June day, my family arrived at the University of Kansas to watch me graduate, which would happen as soon as I paid an enormous library fine. While I was taking my final final, my family luxuriated in the Hallmark Inn swimming pool. It was early in the afternoon, and they had the pool to themselves.

My sister Jenny was about seven years old, and as seven-year-olds sometimes do while swimming, she accidentally drank too much pool water, and out came a rather substantial burp. Her oldest sister, Cathy, heard it, which instantly activated her gag reflex. She'd always suffered from a weak stomach, so it wasn't a complete shock that within ten seconds her entire lunch made a surprise reappearance on her chaise longue.

My sister Lisa, who had her feet dangling in the pool, turned to see what was happening and understandably got instantly grossed out. She puked into the pool. Then, as if Hollywood was scripting it, my sister Ann, who had been under-water, came up for air, right where Lisa had puked. Seeing her sister covered with debris prompted both sister Jenny, the original belcher, and Ann, who now had a vomit halo, to hurl. My mom, the proud matriarch of the clan, completed the royal flush by doing a little heave-ho into the deep end. Naturally, they did what any other decent self-respecting American family on vacation would do—they left without telling anybody what havoc they'd wreaked.

Within half an hour the pool was closed. For a week.

MR. HAPPY'S ADVICE

When traveling with kids, never seat a frequent crier next to a frequent flier.

When traveling by car, make certain you have plenty of games, snacks, and motion-sickness bags for the entire party. If in doubt about any signage, ask the locals what it means, especially you, Diesel.

When you're traveling by air, I suggest using an airline with onboard tele-

visions, so your progenies can be entertained by SpongeBob SquarePants and likely won't pull any of Abe Lincoln's body parts.

Finally, when the beverage cart pulls up, order two cocktails. They might not make it back to you this flight. Besides, the people around you won't think you're a drunk; they can see you're traveling with animal-challenged kids.

"Mooo."

ALMOST RUBBED OUT BY RUDOLPH

Freak Accidents

As a parent, you'll do anything to keep your kids safe and in one piece. So imagine our surprise when our oldest was almost taken out by a cheeseburger, and our youngest was almost whacked by Rudolph the Reindeer.

It was a school holiday, and rather than grilling cheese sandwiches or nuking bean burritos at home, my wife was treating the kids to a sit-down lunch at a fast-food joint in our town. Two of them had ordered the kids' menu item that on this day included nuggety chicken parts, a fistful of French fries, and the real reason they'd come here—a toy. Actually it was a figurine from an animated film they hadn't seen, which immediately segued to "Why don't you take us to the movie after lunch?," which was not on the agenda and had my wife wondering why the restaurant didn't have something useful and educational for the kids to amuse themselves with like a list of state capitals or the major exports of Canada.

My son had graduated to Big Boy food, a fact he reveled in as he croaked out his order in that squeaky growing-boy voice. But after the first bite his voice wasn't croaking, it was choking, as he made the international hand signal for "**Momma,** I've swallowed a Swiss Army knife… and it's open!"

My wife, the action-figure heroine in our family, jumped into gear. With her left hand she cradled his throat so he stopped wiggling, and with her right hand she made a hook with the little finger and quickly removed a mouthful of burger debris. Landing on the tray's paper liner, the culprit was easy to spot. It was a brownish razor-sharp hunk of wood about an inch and a half long and an inch wide.

"Open up, lemme look in your mouth," Dr. Mom instructed the victim. And there on the roof of his mouth was a bright red puncture wound that had not been there pre-burger.

My wife, a Food Network regular viewer, knew that there wasn't supposed to be uncooked wood shrapnel in this particular recipe. She immediately told the others to stop what they were eating, and marched the bloody wood hunk to the boss.

"Are you all right?" would have been the appropriate response from the manager in the paper hat, but instead he listened to my wife and then looked at my bloody boy.

"That's funny, you don't look like a wood-chuck!" He paused for the laughter. "Get it. Woodchuck, he ate wood…"

Clearly a recent graduate of the chain's humor-management team, he listened as my wife demanded an immediate cessation of all food consumption so that all the other sandwich items could be tested for wood bits.

"I can't do that."

"Why not?"

"Just can't."

My wife turned toward the scattered tables and said in a loud voice you'd associate with a flight attendant instructing a planeload of passengers that they were about to ditch into the Indian Ocean, "My son just bit into a cheeseburger and there was a really sharp piece of wood in it. Look at your burgers. There could be more."

Half of them momentarily stopped, lifted the top flap of bun, saw nothing, and resumed their meal. Some did nothing. One threw hers in the garbage, and another clearly hoped that he'd find a shard of wood as well—he took it apart atom by atom, no doubt thinking that if a woman could be awarded millions for a lapful of hot coffee at Wendy's, a wooden spear in a sandwich was certainly worth a Lexus. Disappointed, he found nothing.

Sensing this could turn into a legal problem for his franchise, the manager tried to make it right. "Let me get your son a new cheeseburger."

"Are you crazy?" my wife snapped. "You just turned us all into vegans!"

"How about if I give him a free ice cream?"

That was the last straw. "One sundae, are you nuts? I have three kids!"

She turned and evacuated the children from the franchise and then relocated them to the emergency room of our nearby hospital. After the tetanus shot, and the filing of an official police report, a call was made to a famous TV attorney who made some scary calls to the chain's corporate office. A sum of money was offered to settle the score. My wife just wanted an apology. It never arrived. But a check did, and it was eventually deposited in my son's college account, immediately outsizing my contributions from the previous five years. "Maybe you could gum some mulch and put your sisters through college," I suggested to him, only to meet with an icy stare.

As tragic as it is for a family to be terrorized by fast food, it's worse when a symbol of their favorite holiday almost sends them to that big North Pole in the sky. Our youngest baby girl had developed a high fever. My wife had tried to get her temperature down, but nothing was working. She phoned the pediatrician, who instructed her in an urgent voice to bring her in immediately.

"You'd better keep an eye on her," the nurse said. "The baby could go into convulsions."

"Keep an eye on her" was a problematic request. If the baby went into convulsions in the backseat, my wife wouldn't see it happen. So she did the only thing she could, and she strapped the baby into the front passenger seat, which meant if the air bag deployed, the kid would be launched like a mortar through our back windshield into the radiator grill of any tailgaters.

The pediatrician's office was fifteen miles away, and to get there she'd have to drive some of the most congested and tricky roads in America. So she drove slowly. And carefully. She made sure that no other car would get close to her. She was about three miles from the clinic when the absolute last thing in the world that you'd expect happened. Out of nowhere a head-on collision. That is, a real live deer fell on top of her vehicle.

Yes, on. She had just driven under an overpass, and **boom**! The deer had been on the overpass and either fell, was hit by another car and hurled onto ours, or committed suicide.

Amazingly, because it was an aerial attack, the air bags didn't deploy. But the deer cracked the windshield and caved in the hood. Eighteen inches from the baby's head was a bloody cloven-hoof imprint. Now my wife had two problems, major body damage and a child with a life-threatening fever, but she wasn't going to let some stinking flying deer keep her from getting her baby to the doctor. The SUV was barely drivable, but it made it successfully to the pediatrician's office, where it was determined the baby had one of those mystery illnesses that went away after three days of syringing pink medicine down her hatch.

Our vehicle had $9,700 damage from a deer that nobody but my wife saw. Seconds after the impact, she'd pulled into the breakdown lane and noticed that a car had pulled over behind her. She waited for the Good Samaritan to come to her window; instead the man behind her picked up the dead deer and dumped it into his trunk. He never asked how she or the baby was. He just drove off with the evidence. The ultimate roadkill.

When my wife started the claims process with our insurance company, she was incensed by the line of questioning the agent took.

"So you say the deer came from the sky?"

"Yes."

"And where is the deer now? Did it fly back into the sky?"

"Can I speak with your supervisor?"

Then she'd recount the whole ordeal again from scratch. After five calls and numerous faxes, an adjuster was dispatched to view the carnage.

"Yep, that's a deer hoof," he said as he plucked a chunk of hair out of the wiper blades. He'd seen many a bout between car and deer; car always won. There was no problem after that. A check was cut, the damage was repaired, life went on. About a month later, a quality-control agent from the insurance company called to ask if we were satisfied with their response, and after my wife recounted how there had been some difficulty explaining what had happened, the agent confessed that a supervisor had flagged this case on the first day as a story they wanted to tell at the company Christmas party. "This is the best one this year," he said.

Oh, those crazy actuaries.

Let's go back to the evening of the accident for just a moment. When my wife returned home, she looked like she'd been through the worst day of her life. And she really had. Always the kidder, I tried to inject a little humor into an otherwise awful day. "What's it feel like to kill Rudolph the Red-Nosed Reindeer?"

My son overheard and burst into tears. "Mommy! You killed Rudolph?"

"No," she assured him, "It was Vixen."

MR. HAPPY'S ADVICE

Never place a baby in the front seat of a car under any circumstances.

Never joke about rubbing out one of Santa's reindeer in front of a child.

Hamburgers are safer when run through a blender.

MY FATHER THE SPY, MY MOTHER THE MURDERER

What Parents Do for Their Kids

I would do **anything** for my kids. Before you answer, "So would I," let me ask you a hypothetical question. Let's say your beautiful daughter tried out for the high school cheerleading squad, but didn't make it. The only way she'd get on the squad was if one of the girls dropped out. Most girls don't drop out—unless they're murdered.

That's the story of the Positively True Adventures of the Alleged Texas Cheerleader-Murdering Mom. A Texas mother, Wanda Holloway, tried to hire a hit man to kill one of her daughter's classmates and her mother—because the girl had made cheerleader. Wanda was arrested before anybody got hurt. I'd imagine the story was an inspiration to the squad. "Two, four, six, eight; whose mom do we really hate…"

I would never kill somebody under any circumstances, despite the fact that I live in New Jersey and I have a shovel and a bag of lime in my trunk. But I've got this friend who lost his mind shortly after his daughter entered high school.

It started when she asked if he'd give her a ride. She had a boyfriend. Most girls do. One thing that is universal about high school girls with boyfriends is that when their boyfriends are not with them, they are positive that they are cheating on them, with a much cuter girl who is wearing a much shorter skirt than anything her parents will allow her to appear in outside the home. "We'll just drive by his house to see why he's not answering his phone," she explained. She wanted to make sure the car of a rival girl wasn't parked out front.

"Sure," the Father of the Year said. "Let's go!"

Personally I would have said, "Don't be silly, he's not a cheater, now go get Daddy's paper and slippers." But that's me.

When they drove past the boyfriend's house, they found nothing—no car, no other girls, no nothing. They drove home.

A few nights later: "Dad could you drive me by his house?"

Why not? Dad rationalized. "It's not against the law to drive by…"

Once again they saw nothing. "Where is he?" they wondered. You know the expression "Paranoia will destroy ya?" Paranoia soon started gnawing at both of them. She was miserable, positive something bad was happening behind her back, and her father felt terrible that his little girl was hurting inside.

So this father, who had never been a Navy Seal or a member of the Green Berets but did once spend the night in a Holiday Inn Express, developed a plan: Operation Boyfriend.

After a quick trip down to the local bank he had a map of their entire town. He drew a grid on it. They would systematically travel to "locations of interest." One by one they would eliminate the boyfriend's friends' houses, pool halls, pizza joints, the homes of ex-girlfriends, and the pads of assorted girls who he'd been flirty with. It wasn't scorched earth, it was more scorned.

His SUV would be their mobile command post. It was the perfect covert car, because it was black and would be hard to see as they went trolling the neighborhood. It also had a really good sound system that they'd turn up loud to sing along with the girls of TLC as they belted out "Creep," a cheery little tune about a girl who knows her man is cheating on her. So there they were in a jeep, singing about a creep, which would eventually make her weep. They also had a glove compartment stuffed with Kleenex.

Meanwhile a biographical sketch of the boyfriend was impressive. Good grades, nice person, never in trouble with the law. Sadly, he'd gotten tangled up with a girl whose screwy father had made it his after-work mission to track down his daughter's boyfriend.

This went on for weeks, until they came to a fork in the road. After many miles traveled, they had not found him doing anything embarrassing. Maybe this was a bad idea and they should stop, they thought; besides, what if they did find him doing something naughty? But retreating is for losers, so they kicked it up a bit. They started dressing completely in black like cat burglars. That way, they reasoned, they'd be harder to spot by blabbermouth neighbors once they left the confines of the vehicle. That's right, in phase two she'd be on foot, tiptoeing right up to his window, trying to get a visual confirmation of any hanky-panky.

The paranoid-parade topper was accomplished with a quick trip to Radio Shack, where the father bought the cheapest set of walkie-talkies they sold. "Now when we split up," he said, they could talk while they stalked. Over time it mutated from simple surveillance to something more social. They'd stop by the local Quik Shop for candies, Cokes, and other snack foods to sustain them during their undercover work.

They also started taking her friends along.

"It's so cool, what your dad is doing!" the friends would coo. Their fathers were so boring.

They were reliable men, with developed senses of appropriateness. Not one of them could pull together a cat-burglar costume if his stock portfolio depended on it.

Inexplicably, this dressing in black, driving down alleys with the headlights off, and talking in code continued for the rest of the school year. And the year after that, and the year after that. Every couple of weeks, she'd say, "Let's ride tonight," and Dad would fill up his truck and they'd hit the road.

Today that girl is a woman who lives many miles away from her father. The father is nostalgic for those giggle-filled nights of yesteryear. While hundreds of gallons of fossil fuels were consumed in their quest, not once did they ever find her boyfriend doing anything other than being a perfect gentleman.

But that doesn't mean their mission was a failure. On the contrary, I think it was a complete success. As you examine the genesis of this story, it started as an appeal from a daughter—"Help me, Daddy"—and he did. His career had taken him away from home for long stretches of time, and this was his way to have some one-on-one quality time with his daughter before she grew up and moved out.

"I guess that's really weird," my friend admitted.

Actually, I'm jealous. When my children move away one day, I hope I'll have a story like his. Something I did just one-on-one with each of them. Something fun that we'll remember forever.

Right now I'm confident I won't ever spy on their boyfriends, but there's always the chance one will try out for cheerleader...and not make the squad...

MRS. HAPPY'S ADVICE

If you're considering spying, remember, when purchasing cat-burglar ensembles, brown is the new black.

BE PREPARED

Girl and Boy Scouts

"Hey, Thin Mints, when's the delivery?" barked a very famous guy to the author of this book as they passed at the elevator bank.

"Next Monday," I promised.

"If you've got any spares, I'll buy 'em."

I deceptively gave him an affirmative nod even though I knew there would be no spares. I was bringing exactly as many boxes of Girl Scout cookies in to work as my daughter had sold. 307.

All right, **she** didn't actually sell them; I did. But she did write her name on the bottom of the order form, which was passed pod to pod, office to office. That's the good thing about Girl Scout cookies—they sell themselves. They're that good. Trust me, if the Manson family sold cookies that tasty, most of America would buy them. But the Mansons apparently had no interest in getting involved in the world's largest cookie cartel, the Girl Scouts of America.

At the end of the day, I had to send out a companywide e-mail stating, "The cookie drive is over, please return the form ASAP."

Two days and two more reminders later, it was back in my hands. There are few things in life as gratifying to a young Scout as seeing how many total strangers support scouting. Actually, most weren't supporting the Scouts at all, they were just hooked on the mystical quality of the Girl Scout cookie. It's a taste of our childhood, like the smell of fresh-cut grass and peanut-butter-and-banana sandwiches (everybody goes through an Elvis phase).

All three of my children were at one time or another in the Boy or Girl Scouts. Both programs teach children vital lessons in character, courtesy, and how to hawk stuff.

We were told early on that exotic campouts would be financed through the sale of tons of useless stuff to friends and family members.

As a young Scout, I myself learned the importance of developing a persuasive sales pitch, which would be critical if making a cold call to a neighbor I'd seen only on Halloween. Back in the mid-sixties, my customers in Salina, Kansas, were more than happy to buy whatever we were selling. Unlike the Girl Scouts, who had their trademark cookies, our pack was like eBay in a uniform. We sold everything. Allow me to qualify that: we sold whatever our Scout leader, a very successful father in the food-service industry, could buy in bulk.

For two years we sold Westinghouse lightbulbs. I was the troop's number one salesman. I'd like to think that people bought my bulbs because they were supporters of the Scout program. Given the benefit of hindsight, I now believe many bought just to get me off their porch without incident. I sold hundreds of units of a new-to-the-market-place lightbulb that had three intensities, low, medium, and high. My pitch was so innocent but, upon reflection, so wrong: "Would you be interested in a three-way?"

"Yes, I am," I heard with great frequency.

Given the benefit of time and distance, I wonder how many were disappointed that when they answered in the affirmative, I'd immediately pull out an order form and make a notation. "How many three-ways are you interested in?"

It was the sixties, a time of free love and multiple bulb intensities. I sold a ton.

The next year we sold Christmas cards, but the card stock was flimsy and the artwork made it look like Santa had a five o'clock shadow; nobody wants to send loved ones cards of their favorite elf looking like he's been on a two-week bender.

Sales stank. Inexplicably, we switched to frozen foods, which of course were available at every grocery store in America. So why should anyone purchase flash-frozen peas and carrots from a well-intentioned Boy Scout who did not have a freezer compartment on his bike, at a price double what the local IGA charged? They didn't. It was another tactical error.

Nobody joins the Scouts to become a salesman; they join for the camaraderie and the chance to wear a patch-heavy uniform, and it was the only way my mother would allow me to possess a twenty-seven-function jackknife.

"It'll cut a beer can in half!" I exclaimed.

"Is that what you want to do, cut beer cans in half?" my mom cross-examined.

Actually, I wanted to use a magnifying glass to explode the guts of grasshoppers and other large bugs, but sadly, they weren't in season. Besides, at our first campout, a jackknife provided the most entertainment. Boys away from their mothers **all** spend hours flinging knives through the air in hopes that they'll stick to trees and the sides of outhouses. But on this campout, one of the leaders (who apparently had consumed many an adult beverage) called the boys to gather 'round and watch him cut a Schlitz can in half. That was before the thin-skinned aluminum can had become popular, and real tin was tough to cut. He sawed back and forth with his jackknife until he successfully severed it in half. A cheer went up as he tossed it into the darkened woods behind us.

Approximately three hours later, near 2 A.M., the same leader located at least one half of the tin can with his bare foot. I don't know exactly how deep the can went in, I just know the scream was heard as far south as Camp Mary Dell, where a friend later asked me, "What happened, were you executing a schnauzer?"

That leader was supposed to teach us about "lashings" at nine the next morning, but because he never returned to camp, another father taught us the tenets of campfire safety.

The Scout program was good for me because it gave me an idea of what it was like to live away from home. It was precollege, with bugs and snakes. We had a weekend campout every month of the year, and each summer our leaders would plan the ultimate annual camping trip, two weeks on the edge of a vast cow pasture. During the day we'd learn the fine arts of precision hatchet tossing, river canoeing, and making smoke signals. All good leisure-time activities, but most of us came back year after year for the most dangerous of all scouting activities, riflery.

Twenty-two-caliber guns aimed at paper targets a hundred feet from Scouts down in the dirt on their bellies. A huge dirt berm twenty feet tall kept us from killing the wheat farmer on the other side. It was the most dangerous thing I ever did before I got married. As a fond memory of that camp, I tacked to my bulletin board a paper target with my best shot ever, a bull's eye; it remained there, until the day I went to college, to remind me that if needed, I could defend myself when armed. I would have shown it at school, but the Vietnam War was winding down at the time, and I didn't want to be the first fifth-grader to be drafted.

"He's a crack shot," the GI recruiter told my mom in my dream. "Ma'am, his country needs him."

"But he's needed stateside to sell lightbulbs," she begged, until I woke up in the same sweat as I do after the dream in which I show up at work without pants.

Scouting also taught me the lessons of character and economy. I remember visiting the latrine after a disturbing breakfast of uncooked oatmeal flakes, brown sugar, and raisins, drowned in an eighth of a cup of Carnation evaporated milk. When I arrived, there was not one atom of toilet paper remaining, so I went to the quartermaster, who apparently was under orders to reduce Charmin usage.

"We just put three rolls in there. Are you sure they're gone, Scout?"

"Yes sir," I replied in my clipped premilitary voice.

"How much are you using? A whole handful or just one sheet?"

Just one sheet? Was he nuts? I was more of a half-a-roll user. But the Scouts demanded truth and honesty above all else. "Just one sheet, sir."

"It must be those boys from Troop 219," he said as he issued me three additional rolls, then turned to record the withdrawal in the Official Toilet Paper Inventory Report. I returned to the latrine with two of the rolls; the other I kept under my cot, in the event of nosebleeds, hay fever, or another breakfast of uncooked Quaker Oats.

By the end of my scouting career, I'd learned how to tie knots, sell things, look good in a uniform, and have plenty of unsupervised fun.

So when my second-grade son came home with the sign-up sheet for scouting, I was delighted. Finally we'd have an exclusive father-son event. He signed up, and I was ready to relive those days of yesteryear.

Later that month he pledged to "obey the laws of the pack" and we were in. After they taught him the handshake, he received his first assignment: sell popcorn.

Unlike other Scouts who didn't bother to even try to sell any, my son made an effective sales pitch to my wife, who promptly bought the required twenty units of popcorn.

"I'm going to the campout!" my son squealed. We had popcorn for two years.

Headed for the hills, I signed up to chaperone. Because my father had not been a Scout leader or even a volunteer, I was unfamiliar with the adult logistics of campouts. As it turned out, each of the ten fathers making the trip would be responsible for one of the major food groups. I was Mr. Weiner. My wife carefully packed six dozen all-beef franks on ice in the back of the Explorer and sent us on our way.

When we were halfway to our destination, a terrible late-spring thunderstorm came up and made the trip scary.

"Do you think it's raining at the camp, Dad?"

Being a professional in the weather business, I leveled with him. "No idea."

When we arrived at the campground, the heavens were hemorrhaging and my son witnessed his first cloudburst. It was terrifying. Thunder, lightning, and an absolute wall of water. I asked an Eagle Scout in an adjacent vehicle if he'd lash together an ark.

"What about the bark?" he hollered over the rain.

Noah humor apparently didn't work during an actual storm of biblical proportions.

Thirty minutes later the rain slowed to the point that we could drag our stuff to our campsite. It was muddy and dark, and the only time we could clearly see where we were was during a lightning strike, when we moved fast. According to the running ink of my copy of the base-camp diagram, this was the spot.

I located a bit of a clearing, and there on what I'd estimate was a thirty-degree grade, where the runoff formed little rivers on the forest floor, we'd homestead. I'd purchased the tent the day before at Costco, mainly because it said on the box, "Assembles in less than two minutes." Perfect—a tent for the short-attention-span camper.

I threaded two cross poles through a flap at the top, then used one of my Merrills to drive four stakes into the squishy ground. Approaching the two-minute mark, I released one doohickey and the tent popped up, ready to move into.

The deafening roar of the rain masked the sounds of the wild animals that were certainly nearby, ready to claw our eyes out. But because it was now raining in squalls, they were taking a raincheck on eating us in our sleep.

The next morning, I realized that sleeping with my feet running up the thirty-degree hill had drained the blood from my legs and now it was pooling in my head. I woke up feeling my heart beating like Big Ben in my thighs.

Outside I discovered some good news and some bad news. The good news: another father had already risen and brewed up a tankard of

Maxwell House. The bad news: I was in some-body else's campsite. I was in the right location, and yet our entire pack was missing. The wind and the rain, the tornado warning, and the light-ning had scared them from making the trip. But ours wasn't the only pack of Nancys, 90 percent of those who'd signed up didn't show up.

Of our pack, just two families made the trip. As you know, we were in charge of the hot dogs. But the bun family didn't show, and the condi-ment dad wasn't there. Chips and beans were both MIA. The other dad who did show was in charge of the off-the-books item: beer.

The boys thought it was fun having cold wein-ers for every meal. (The guy with the camp stove and matches hadn't made it either.) I had a case of apple juiceboxes in my truck from soccer prac-tice, so the boys had plenty to wash down the weenies.

Meanwhile, the father who'd brought the beer had brought enough for ten guys. Don't worry, we didn't drink it all ourselves. Our sons watched with great capitalistic interest as we used our beer cache to barter with some other nearby fathers who had things we needed for our survival. If you're curious, a six-pack of Coors Light is an even trade for a king-sized bag of Cool Ranch Doritos.

And despite that voluminous beverage con-sumption, I never strayed from the tent in the middle of the night, because visions from twenty-five summers earlier of a bloody Scout leader hopping around on one foot still haunted me. I'd hold it till sunup.

Two years later my son dropped out of the Scout program. He had tired of asking his parents to buy his way to camp. It was the end of an era. My scouting days were over, I thought—until my middle girl announced she was joining the Girl Scouts.

Their campouts were doubtless boring in comparison to the boys'. Would they have had a "gas volume competition"? No chance. They probably whiled away the hours swapping stories about school friends and remedies for split ends.

I was useless to my scouting daughter, until she asked if I could help her sell Girl Scout cookies so she could get her cookie merit badge. She'd never asked for my help on a project before, and I jumped at the chance to bond. "I'll take it to work in the morning."

With orders for 307 boxes, many to employees I'd never heard of and didn't know where to find, I drove on a Saturday morning into New York City with a truckload of Thin Mints, Do-Si-Dos, Trefoils, and Savannahs. It took many trips from the ground floor to my office dozens of floors above Rockefeller Center. They were heavy and bulky, and I discovered they were hard to balance as I showed the guard my ID each time I went into the building. "I was just here three minutes ago!" I'd protest.

"ID, please."

On the seventh entrance he realized I was not Al-Qaeda and stopped asking for identification. On my last trip I tipped him a box of Samoas.

It took me two and a half weeks to distribute the cookies.

When I announced to my daughter that I'd distributed all of **her** cookies and had a wad of cash to rival any Vegas gambler's, she said, "Thanks. Do you know where my iPod is?"

That was it?

Twenty-five trips up a freight elevator on my day off, numerous phone calls to seemingly non-existent employees to "pick up your cookies in my office," and "Thanks, where's my iPod?" was all I got?

I didn't really say any of that, because just before my impending heart failure, my daughter came over to me and gave me a hug and a kiss.

"Thanks, Dad."

For a moment I realized why I'd done it all. For my wonderful, beautiful daughter. Just then she put her hand down and retrieved the iPod I'd apparently been leaning against.

Wait a minute.

Had she said, "Thanks, Dad" for the cookies or for locating her iPod? It didn't matter, because unlike those other cookie-selling mothers and fathers, I'd been able to give my daughter something their little girls would never have. The title of Best Salesgirl! For a Girl Scout, it's like getting a Video Music Award.

And what was the grand prize for selling the most cookies?

A towel.

She didn't need a towel, however I needed a truss.

MRS. HAPPY'S ADVICE

I like the Scout programs.

They prepare kids for making ethical and moral choices, by drilling the values of scouting into their heads.

However, if you're going to wind up trafficking cookies/lightbulbs/whatever, at least specify a prize you want. Forget about towels. I'd suggest cash.

The real Scout motto should be: Be prepared, to sell stuff.

THE COACH BAG

Going Out for the Team

Your children will one day announce that they want to "go out for the team." This will be for one of three reasons. Either they enjoy the thrill of athletic competition, or their friends are on the team, or they like to dress up in uniforms with jumbo numbers that can easily be read from the International Space Station.

The dream of every parent who watches their son or daughter suit up is that one day he or she will catch the eye of a college scout, who'll offer a full ride to a fabulous university where your child will play four years until getting drafted by the pros, at which point he or she will earn hundreds of millions of dollars, many of which you hope to quietly siphon off while living in the mansion they buy you next door to P. Diddy.

But the only way they'll go pro, and get that Nike deal, is for their coach to recognize that your child, the future superstar, needs to be put into the game pronto! If your future T-ball-playing Hall of Famer doesn't go in soon, she won't master this sport, which means she won't be good at softball, which means she'll stink at baseball, which means no scholarship deal, no pro bonuses, no life of luxury, and she'll wind up sweeping the floor at Rosie's barbershop.

The two most pressing things on the mind of a parent pacing the sidelines are

1. Why doesn't the coach play my child as much as the other kids?

2. Why did I just drink that extra-large Dunkin' Donuts coffee, knowing there is no Porta Potti here on field 9?

In my town, there is a rule that every child must play half of the game. It's a great rule designed to make the sport inclusive of all, regardless of athletic skill. But a number of my son's coaches, who shall remain nameless for lawsuit purposes, would only put my son in with ninety seconds left in the half or at the end of the game. They thought having him in would jeopardize the outcome of the game. Instead they'd lose with their own child playing in my kid's slot. After seven seasons of humiliation, there was just one thing to do.

I volunteered to coach.

Until that point I'd always felt unqualified to coach. The parent coaches I'd observed all seemed so prepared, with game plans, matching sweatbands, dry-erase boards, and special pylons they'd pull out of their SUVs at 7 A.M. on frighteningly cold Saturday mornings. They seemed to have special coaching knowledge that was only available to **real** coaches. I was a lousy athlete "back in the day" and knew in my heart I was woefully unqualified, and yet I filled out a form and mailed it in, and before I knew it, I was strolling my town's vast stretches of turf with a whistle and wearing an official head-coach shirt. Why did I do it? Two reasons.

1. This would be my son's final year on a town team. My last chance to be his coach. I'd watched so many others bark at him. This was my one and only opportunity. I wanted that special bond that a son has with his father. I wanted him to brag, "My dad's the coach, your dad forgot the snacks!"
2. The only way my son would get into the game for more than ninety seconds was if his coach was a blood relative.

It started with the baseball draft. I knew about 25 percent of the draftees. My intention was to field a team of my son's pals from his school. "Not so fast," said one of the other dads who looked at my list of hopeful players. "I need that kid because he's my son's best friend," he told me and the assembled others. Turns out they weren't really pals, but the other father desperately wanted the kid with the eighty-four-mph slider, so lying about social ties was not a mortal sin.

The players would be selected much as they are in the pros. The first choice went to the coach whose son was rated the worst player by his coach the year before. The last chore of the previous season was to have the coaches rate the teams. Give every kid a number between 1 and 5. Universally the father/coaches gave their own children 1 ratings—the dad equivalent of awarding your kid an Oscar.

My son was rated by a guy who never played him. Next to my son's name was a 4. At first I felt sorry for him, until they explained that because my son had the lowest rating, I would get the first pick. I chose the best pitcher. Then I got the best shortstop and first baseman. It was all done with numbers; with each boy weighted by his rating, I had to reach a total of 18 by the end of each round. My head was throbbing. They kept explaining it, but I had no idea what I was doing.

Some of the other father coaches had clearly spent hours working on the draft before we started. They had spreadsheets and had worked up the kids' averages over their grade and middle school careers. Me, I didn't know who most of the kids were, but my son had given me a handwritten note of ten names on the back of my Visa bill. I got all but one.

To make sure that I would not be like the coaches who barely played my son, flaunting the rule that every child play half of the game, I used an Excel program and charted every inning, and every child played every position he asked for and spent at least half the game on the field. This was backed up by the parents who sat in the stands and kept their own books to make sure that I was playing their kid the legal minimum.

The season was spectacular. Years later the boys (now college students) would still refer to it as "the Illegal Rec Team," because it was stacked with so many great players. In fact 90 percent of my team would four years later be in the high school state championships. They were all eyeballed by scouts from the pros, and a couple got scholarships for college. Just think of the thousands of dollars in tuition I saved those parents, the same ones who'd tell me I wasn't playing their boys enough or that I'd put them in the wrong position. But it was worth it because in my library proudly stands the runner-up trophy we got from our town's world series. Now that the statute of limitations has run out, I can confess that the secret to our success was easy. Whenever the other team was ahead on the scoreboard, I'd simply announce, "I've got a dollar for the next run."

"How much for a homer, Coach?"

The answer was five bucks. I always paid, including the time I had to borrow a ten from the catcher. (It's always embarrassing when an eighth-grader has more disposable income than you.)

Now the downside: having coached my boy for his farewell season of rec sports, I was asked by my two girls to be their coach. Quid pro coach. So I did just that for four years. In the fall I'd show the girls how to defend the soccer goal while dodging the goose poop, and in the spring I'd show them how to slide into home while dodging the goose poop.

Here's the difference between coaching boys and girls. The boys don't listen to you. They're too busy giggling and giving each other wedgies. Meanwhile, the girls do listen, because they want to know if it's time for a snack.

Coaching eats up vast slabs of your free time. Three hours three times a week minimum, plus the time spent filling out game plans, calling everybody to notify them of field changes and rainouts. And despite all the time you've invested in the sport, many parents treat sports practices and games as child care. You aren't a coach; you're a babysitter until five-thirty. The kids were great. Some of their parents were weenies.

"My daughter can't come to practice, ever," one mother told me. "But you still have to play her half the game, okay?"

"How will she learn the game?" I stupidly asked.

"She's got a DVD I'll play for her in my Astro van after ballet class but before cheerleading."

Another mother knew that practice was over at six, yet she never arrived for pickup before six-thirty. Each time she'd lower her electric window to say "Sorry."

She wasn't sorry; she had a spinning class that she "just couldn't miss." She was treating me like a servant. I'd have been happy to be her servant, but only if I got dental benefits and a car allowance.

Some of the other team's volunteer dads, I discovered, were not there to teach the fundamentals of the game; they were there to make sure their kids beat the soup out of our team, at any cost. In a playoff game one coach heckled my daughter, who was pitching at the time. "Girls, don't worry about her, she can't get it across the plate. She's terrible!" Later he followed up with "Is that the best you can do, honey?" Then he let out a hardy-har-har laugh.

My daughter showed great poise, finished the inning, retired the side, and we won. But as she walked off the diamond, she burst into tears. Coach Bigmouth had wrecked it for her forever. It was the last time she'd ever pitch a ball. I saw that coach the next day, in church. I know it was wrong for me to hope that a lightning bolt would kill him on the spot, but sometimes a guy's mind wanders during the sermon.

I also took exception to the opinion of an assistant coach who made a frank assessment: "Our girls aren't very good." I reminded him we weren't there to win, we were there to teach our daughters how the game is played and have some fun. He nodded. "Yeah, but they still suck."

Another year an irate coach/father screamed a stream of expletives my way. This while he was seated on the bench, next to his team of girls. They were horrified. When I asked him to step out of the dugout to chat about it, he threatened to whack me. I wasn't really scared, although I did have my centerfielder start my car whenever we'd play that team. Luckily the parents of the girls on his team complained, and he was mysteriously not accepted as a coach the following year.

I am currently retired from the coaching business. My son has graduated and gone off to college, and his sisters both play lacrosse, a wonderful sport where they run up and down the field hitting each other with sticks. My eldest daughter has already broken her ankle and nose. She's also good with the stick, which will come in handy if she ever sees that bigmouth coach who heckled her years before.

Looking back, I loved the time I spent with my kids. It also gave them a special status with the others. They always got to start the game, and they'd ask me to put their friends on the field close to them, so during the dull times they could chitchat away.

I also miss the final game of the season when the girls would present a game ball signed by them and a card of thanks signed by their parents, who barely knew me except to scold me about playing my daughter more than theirs.

"You're right, I am," I'd say. "It's the **one** benefit of being the coach."

Like clockwork at the next-to-last game of the season, one of the well-intentioned mothers would hit up the other parents for five bucks to buy the coach a farewell gift. Usually the gift was a bottle of wine. Finally, I had something in common with the parents. Their kids had driven us all to drink.

MRS. HAPPY'S ADVICE

If your children want to go out for a team, support them. It's really good exercise, and with any luck, by the end of the game they'll be exhausted and sleep soundly when the R-rated movie on Cinemax is about to start.

Do not yell at the volunteer coaches. Most are doing the best they can. If they wanted to get berated, they would have stayed at work.

THE GRADUATE

Kids and College

You've scrimped and saved, you've carried a lunch to work, and you've turned off the lights when you left the room, just so one day that high school student who barely talks to you can be transported from the squalor that is his room to a college or university much more prestigious than the joint from which you graduated.

But before they leave, they have to decide where they want to blow your life's savings. Surprisingly, they couldn't care less. When I asked my son, he wondered how hard it would be to get into the College of Cardinals.

"Generally, you have to be a priest."

"Scratch that," my son thought. "Priests work weekends."

"How about Notre Dame?" he asked. That of course is a wonderful university steeped in tradition. It would be perfect. The reason he picked it was because the night before on Starz we'd watched the movie **Rudy**. When I ran into Sean Astin, the actor who played the title role in the movie, he said he would write a letter on my son's behalf. In South Bend the two biggest names are Rudy and Regis, and who knows, a one-page note from a **Lord of the Rings** star might help. Besides, he's not Regis's son...I don't think.

In the early spring of my son's junior year, we called over a family friend, Giles, who's a college counselor, and over a quiche lorraine and fruit salad, he reviewed my son's GPA, SAT scores, and extracurriculars.

After an agonizing five minutes where he sat lasered to the papers, he returned this verdict to my boy. "Son, your wife is not at Notre Dame."

It seemed like an odd thing to tell a seventeen-year-old, but when you think about it, it was actually brilliant. If a young man is going to invest four years of his life in a place, why not do it where there are cute girls? But where?

Thus began a yearlong odyssey that started with the selection of twenty possible schools. Next we mapped out three road trips that my wife and son would make over the next three months. The northern route would take us to Massachusetts and New York schools, a southern route through Maryland and Virginia, and finally we'd go west, young man, and check out Pennsylvania.

College tours work like this: you go to a school, listen to an admissions official tell you how fabulous its program is, and then a student guide does the legwork and shows you around. The guides really make or break a school. One engineering student at a college with two proper names, much like William & Mary, said, "I don't know why I wound up coming here, because confidentially, I hate it!"

At another school a girl guide in a painfully tight belly shirt didn't talk about academics or social life; instead she focused on the university's food choices and how she loved to shop off campus at Wawa. "Send me cookies and candy and cards," she instructed the parents as the tour concluded. Scratch.

While my wife and I would ask about meal plans and "how many quarters is the dryer," our son had just one question: "What do you do for fun around here?"

"There's a very active bar scene just off campus," one guide revealed. "Tuesday night is Dime

Beer Night." Scratch that, Tuesday nights are for studying, not looking for loose change.

My son wasn't very interested in the school where the accounting major made a pitch for him to join the Math Club. He'd spent four years in high school avoiding the mathletes; he would not spend the next four years paying to hang with them.

In the early running one school emerged as my son's hands-down favorite. Was it the variety of programs, the storied faculty, the impressive athletic teams? Not really. He was more fascinated by the gorgeous pre-med coed who gave the tour.

Giles was right, my son's future wife wasn't at Notre Dame, she was here, walking backward. He was officially in love...with that school.

By the end of December, it was time to start submitting the college applications and essays. Meanwhile, the parents have a role as well, contacting every friend or relative with even the slightest connection to the college, calling in all markers, trying to get the tiniest extra edge. Let the brownnosing begin!

But it's hard to get a kid in senior year to focus on anything so far in the future. Remember, this is a special time in his life when he and his classmates are consumed with inventing ways to shoot Silly String at graduation.

Through sheer willpower and occasional intimidation—"If you want to use the car, you've got to write your essay"—seven applications were electronically delivered before midnight on December 31.

Now we'd wait. On 7:25 P.M. April 1, I downloaded the first official news, from a really good school with an enormous attitude. "Thanks for applying, but unless your father can build a wing on our future school of economics, drop dead."

An hour later, his first-choice school with the cute pre-med coed weighed in: wait list.

I knew it! We should have **demanded** that they keep score in T-ball! That "it's a tie, we're-all-winners" psychobabble doesn't develop the killer instinct.

And all that back-channeling and backslapping that we thought would help him get an extra edge in the selection process didn't work. For one school, two impressive letters were written on my son's behalf, one by a U.S. senator, who might one day be president, and another by a "legacy" who reminded the dean of admissions he'd just donated one million dollars to the university that week. "Your son is a lock," he told me just before we got the e-mail message from the dean of admissions: "Admission declined."

In the space of two minutes I'd developed a nine-Excedrin-tablet headache. In my mind those dreams of him one day becoming a successful attorney were now careening off the tracks, and he was heading for a weekend job collecting tolls on the New Jersey Turnpike.

"Is there such a thing as college homeschool?" I asked my wife.

Four colleges did eventually send the "big envelope," so he could go somewhere, but he wasn't that crazy about any of them. The most intriguing was a school that accepted him even though he'd never been there: Penn State.

Time for a road trip. A four-hour ride to a place that reminded me of where I went to college. I immediately started remembering all of the fun I had, and of course I hoped one day my son would have similar fun times, without the toga and the girls' glee club.

Because this was an emergency campus tour, we asked the son of a family friend to show him around the sprawling campus, while we ate in a dormitory cafeteria where he would take all of his meals, if he was awake. The Mexican buffet was a nice touch, but the omelet bar seemed extravagant. And the ever-ready soft-serve ice cream machine we knew would seal the deal. This place was perfect.

An hour later, my son reappeared with his tour guide, who was wearing a Miller Time baseball cap. This kid had not given him a tour of the campus but instead took him for a ride past his apartment, through downtown, showed him where the adult-beverage establishments were located, and introduced him to members of his junior-class posse. My son had a huge grin on his face. "I want to go here."

"Hallelujah! Houston, we have a college."

Before we left, we paid all the fees for the upcoming semester, so the university couldn't change its mind. We'd spent the night at the Nittany Lion Inn, where as we were checking out, the man who opened the door for us didn't just look like Joe Paterno, he **was** Joe Paterno.

Think of the symbolism, there was Mr. Penn State, opening the door for MY SON! The only thing that would have made it better would have been for him to say, "You look like a nice kid. Wanna be my starting linebacker? Here's a full-ride scholarship! See you in the fall, kid!"

We were on cloud nine. Until we got home.

The answering machine was blinking. "Hi, it's the dean of admissions at your first-choice college. We see you're on the wait list. As it turns out, we have one chair left. Call by five P.M. and let us know."

I was for the big Joe Paterno school. My wife was for the smaller, more expensive school. As always, my wife won. And once again she was right.

When I told a friend where my son was enrolling, he gave me that "You've got to be kidding" look. "What's the matter?" I asked.

"The only person I know who went to that school was an engineering student who took pictures of every poop he had his freshman year."

I was grossed out but oddly fascinated. "What did he do with the photos?" I asked.

"He showed them to everybody who came to his dorm. It was a real icebreaker."

That, I thought, was the one-in-a-million freak, who gave that school a bad name. My son would attend this school and leave his mark on the place, at least that's how I rationalized it as my wife dropped off our son at his dream college for a three-day orientation in mid-August. She called me as she was trying to exit, but she was stuck in a traffic jam, surrounded by other parents who'd also just dropped off their children.

"Everybody in every car is crying," she whispered.

"He'll be back," I assured her. "He needs stuff. He needs us." I hoped I was right, even though I knew the future was a crapshoot.

"Kids grow up and then they leave," my dad told me on the day I went off to college. That was thirty years ago. I talk to him on the phone all the time, but I never moved back home.

As I closed my eyes, something weird happened. In my mind's eye I could see my college freshman carrying his stuff into his dorm, but instead of hearing his voice as it was that day, I heard a scream from eighteen years earlier after the doctor slapped him on the butt and our son entered our lives. Grown-up boy, baby voice.

I was hallucinating a little bit, but we'd all been under a lot of pressure. We'd spent so much time hounding him to get good grades, so he could get into a great school, and now he was at one. That made me feel good until Parents' Weekend, when I attended a workshop on how to plan your child's classes to make him attractive to future employers.

That's when it hit me. I'd just spent four years getting him into a school, and now I was going to spend the next four years getting him a good job. Does Sean Astin need an assistant? I've got his e-mail somewhere…

MRS. HAPPY'S ADVICE

For nearly two decades, you've encouraged and explained, given them answers to their questions, some of which you made up just to shut them up.

You've done a lot of talking. And despite the fear of "the sex talk," I know with great certainty the hardest thing in the English language that a parent will ever say to their kid: Good-bye.

chapter five

Mature Topics

WHERE DO I PLUG THIS IN?

Appliances

This is not a sex book. And I'm not a doctor, but I play one at home. However, there are readers who are interested in knowing the ins and outs of this topic, so to speak.

Considering that what I have to say will be analyzed by everyone from Dr. Phil to my parish priest, let me describe sex as any normal handyman would: in appliance terms.

Men are like microwave ovens; women are like Crock-Pots.

Fast, furious, done lickety-split, versus slow, methodical, concluding later that same day.

Microwave versus Crock-Pot.

Who's hungry for takeout?

I LOVE YOU, YOU'RE PERFECT, NOW WEAR THIS THONG

Do Not Attempt This at Home

Some things should never be attempted, like doing karaoke sober.

There's a chance that your spouse has in the back of her head a few "fantasies that will happen, now that we're married." Be careful about what line you're willing to cross, and how hard you're willing to push somebody to change. Putting the toothpaste back in the tube is easier than dressing up like Little Bo Peep—I've heard that Bo's bonnet can almost cut off the circulation to the average man's medulla oblongata.

"As I was walking down the aisle, I had the feeling I was marrying the wrong guy," a famous divorcée confessed. "I knew he had some terrible habits, but I thought I could change him. Ten years later I know it's a bad idea to change a person, nor should you try."

Experts say that a person's personality is generally in place by the age of eighteen months. So don't go thinking that through your persuasive personality and helpful suggestions you can create the perfect spouse, unless you got your meat hooks in him when he was still pre-K.

Brainwashing doesn't work. I've tried. The best you can do when you want your beloved to change is nudge.

If he's hitting the sauce too heavy, only go to places where no liquor is served, like the Dalai Lama's. If driving prompts her to fly into road rage, maybe you should offer to chauffer her around town. If he's adopted the bad habit of using really dirty language, invite a nun over for dinner once a week.

I did successfully nudge my wife away from retail, to wholesale. And now it fits our lifestyle. We're simple folk with simple needs. We're not real socialites. We don't belong to a country club. In fact, the only club we belong to is Sam's Club.

Things You Should Never Do After Dark

- Never enter a room that contains a trapeze or a pony unless the word **Flying** is in front of your family name.
- Never put on an item of intimate wear that looks like it will hurt.
- Immediately return any skimpy outfits that appear to have been worn previously by a person less groomed than yourself.

- Never play strip poker with your neighbors or any member of the Knights of Columbus.

THE LOVE MACHINE, BY KENMORE

Mom and Dad Take a Time-out

Kids are like United Nations weapons inspectors: you hear them coming toward you when you're doing something they'd find puzzling, and just as the door swings open and they're about to say "Aha!" you've hidden the yellowcake uranium or the large vibrating egg.

Thanks to their astronomical sugar intake, children are generally always awake. So that creates a problem when one parent desires a few minutes of uninterrupted face time **in private** with his or her spouse during daylight hours. Biologically, you can't turn off your primal urges until your child enters the seminary in fifteen years. So what's a parent to do? Here's a suggestion.

Let's say the children are safely inside the house, watching a television program, playing a game, or quietly scheming about how to torment you later. Your window of opportunity is brief; you must act quickly. First one parent gives the other "the Signal," and they reconvene next to the washing machine and dryer.

1. Locate a pair of heat-resistant tennis shoes.
2. Obtain two or three large fluffy towels.
3. Place both shoes and towels in the dryer.
4. Set the timer for thirty minutes. (Ha!)
5. Go to your sleeping quarters and lock the door.

The meter is now running. Many parents may feel inhibited, knowing that the children are just a few yards away. However, those tennis shoes slamming on the dryer walls are **so loud**, your kids won't hear a peep. Of course if you dawdle, don't be surprised if after a few minutes there is an urgent banging on the door, followed by a set of eyes at floor level, and then the voice of your child, who's looking for her waiter. "Mommy, Daddy, what are you guys doing in there?"

Do not respond. They know you're in there. They will not go away until you come out with your hands up. Take your time in opening the door, because you know exactly what they'll ask, and you'll know how to respond.

"Mommy, why was the door locked?"

You'll skirt the question and ask your own: "What was so urgent you needed to wake Mommy and Daddy from their nap?"

Vegas oddsmakers say there's a three-in-nine chance they'll respond, "I need a glass of water," which you'll automatically fetch and place next to the untouched glass of water that you got them fifteen minutes ago. But getting the glass of water doesn't shut them up; just as with Helen Thomas at a White House press conference, there will be a follow-up.

"Why was your door closed?"

Of course you can't lie to them per se, so instead I suggest a response that has been scientifically proven to shut them up. "Who wants to go to Dairy Queen?"

By the time everybody is in the car, your banging laundry load is completely dry.

PORN LOSERS

When You See Things You Should Not

It was a Friday night, and Mr. and Mrs. Excitement were living the exciting life of suburbanites channel surfing. Nope, **click**, nope, **click**, nope, **click**…STOP! It's porn! Bunches of naked people doing things naked people do. It's really weird watching it on the same TV on which we watch **Finding Nemo**.

"Something's wrong," I told my wife. She agreed. The voice on the screen did not match what we were watching. We heard a slow-and-steady probably older woman speaking of salvation and, oddly, abstinence, but the screen showed a perky blonde who was well on her way to a significant rug burn.

Wait a minute, I recognize that woman's voice! **Click**. I surfed down one cable channel, and there was the same voice, in the body of a nun on EWTN, the Catholic channel. My wife flipped up one number, and sure enough, there were the naked people, but we didn't hear them, we heard only the voice of the sister. How ironic. Anybody who paid money for this stuff **had** to hear about "sins of the flesh" and "eternal damnation." Even though it was hilarious, we turned it off after thirty seconds.

My wife, a CCD teacher, said that if we were getting this free porn by accident, surely there were others getting it too, so to speak. So she went to the kitchen, looked up the number, and called the cable company to complain. For $125 a month you'd think there would be a live person to talk to; instead she left her message at the sound of the beep. "Hi, I'm calling to complain about the naked people with the nun's voice…"

The next day a completely embarrassed customer-service vice president called to apologize. He saw the same thing at his house and felt terrible that we'd accidentally been exposed to it. When he found out my wife was a Sunday-school teacher, I'm certain he said a quiet Hail Mary that he wouldn't wind up in the EZ Pass lane to Hell.

He explained that a computer-software problem was the culprit, scrambling the audio and video portions of the program on different channels. "But it's fixed now," he said, and he promised it would never happen again. My wife asked him how many other cable customers had gotten the same free peep show.

"One point two million homes," he told us.

"And how many called to complain?"

"Just you."

Let's face it; most people would just watch it. They'd reason that there's something very convenient about having the kind of mature entertainment once available only in those dirty bookstores down by the bus depot now live in your living room. Why call and bellyache? Then it might not happen again.

MRS. HAPPY'S ADVICE

Think twice before ordering adult materials. There's always a paper trail, and it could come back to haunt you when you're nominated for Rotarian of the Year.

Most people don't come across accidental free porn like we did. Instead they have to order it. According to what I've read online, there are thousands of husbands and wives who

make their own dirty movies, starring themselves. Do not do this under any circumstances.

Here's why.

One day your children will be innocently looking for the Mary Poppins tape, and when they can't find it, they'll stick in an unlabeled Memorex that simply says "XXX."

"I thought it was the movie XXX: State of the Union! I didn't know you'd be in it naked, Dad!" You never want to have that conversation with a child, relative, or member of building services.

"Daddy, one more thing," your child adds, as the shame fest continues. "You really should shave your back."

ME TARZAN, YOU NEIGHBOR

Swingers

What is the difference between swingers and swappers? I don't know, but I have the feeling there are a few in our neighborhood. They travel together to exotic locations, without their children, where I'm certain they apply cocoa butter to one another in places that burn easily.

The whole scene seems a bit sketchy.

However, I do want to know why, if they are swingers or swappers, they haven't hit on my wife or me. What's the matter with us? Why don't they want us for their triangle? Or quadrangle? I'll tell you why. Because we are squares. And we're planning to keep it that way.

But at least they **could ask.**

MRS. HAPPY'S ADVICE

If somebody approaches you to join a "special club," you may be motivated to immediately move from your town. Someday you will see that person again, and when you do, you'll think, "Swapper." It's like an invisible tattoo across their forehead that only you can see.

If you tell your spouse about being approached, and your spouse thinks it's a good idea, you've got some serious problems. She could just be testing you to see what you would say. Or producers could be taping an upcoming episode of Candid Camera.

chapter six

Troubleshooting

This chapter is to help with some unforeseen problems that may arise during the course of your marriage.

KILL HIM WITH KINDNESS

Desperate Housewives

Lorena Bobbitt couldn't take it anymore, and to her there was only one solution: as her husband, John Wayne Bobbitt, slept, she cut off several inches of his penis.

I think the average man would have noticed the carving sensation and woken up, but apparently Mr. Bobbitt was a very sound sleeper. He didn't arise, so to speak, until the little woman had already driven off and thrown her fistful of trouble out the window. That was an all-points bulletin local law enforcement didn't hear every day. "Attention all cars: be on the lookout for a severed penis!"

Thousands of square miles to search, and one eagle-eyed patrolman spotted the missing part. Thanks to a medical miracle, they rushed it into a waiting operating room and reattached it to Mr. Bobbitt.

His wife was eventually charged with "malicious wounding." After the jury heard testimony, they bought her argument that she had acted on an "irresistible impulse" and she was found not guilty. She was ordered to spend forty-five days in a mental hospital, where I'm sure the male nurses kept their distance.

I know of another woman who had tired of her husband, so just like the Roadrunner going after Coyote, she smacked him upside the head with a cast-iron skillet.

He lived; she was arrested. They both hired Acme Attorneys, and now they're divorced and big Zoloft consumers.

Both of these stories involve blunt-force trauma. But the most diabolical example of the **perfect** crime didn't involve a pawnshop pistol or a steak knife from Ponderosa.

The husband and wife had lived their entire lives in a Norman Rockwell town in New England, members of an Arnold Palmer–designed golf course, unquestionably both pillars of their community. They personified one of those Morgan Stanley ads, where retirement looks so perfect, you can hardly wait to start showing up for the early bird specials.

But at home, he'd been pestering her, for decades. She got to the point of no return. Their country club did not allow divorcées as members. If Dick divorced Jane, neither would remain a member. (The Kennedys need not apply.) However, if Dick died, Jane the widow could continue, and would doubtless be envied by the other miserable housewives when she wasn't being hit on by the club pros.

Divorce was not an option; that left only murder. She hatched her plot after watching something on TV. No, it wasn't **America's Most Wanted,** or **Cops,** or **CSI: Miami**. It was a show on Food Network. Halfway through a Valentine's Day baron o' beef recipe, the TV chef reminded viewers, "Ladies, remember, the fastest way to a man's heart is through his stomach." Jackpot!

After her husband's second heart attack, a cardiologist made it clear to both of them that he would die unless he immediately started on a very restricted diet. No red meat, low-salt, and absolutely NO BUTTER. She had followed the recipes perfectly, but his after-meal reviews were killing her.

"This tastes like crap." And maybe it did, but she was only doing it for him. It was time to send him to that big diner in the sky. She started buying butter, in bulk. A stocky man with a hair-trigger temper, he'd hit the roof if he found out, so she stored it down in the basement in a mini-refrigerator that one of the kids had brought back from college.

With her first Land O'Lakes–laden entrée, his food complaints stopped immediately.

"This diet stuff isn't half bad," he said with half a mouthful. It shouldn't have been—she'd put an entire stick in the cauliflower mashed potatoes, a whole stick on the salmon, and had even created a salad dressing that was 75 percent liquefied butter, 100 percent trouble.

Within three weeks, he'd gained weight and was starting to wheeze by the time he hit the landing going up the staircase. He was starting to feel a few weird twinges in his chest, and yet he was never late for his diet plate.

He was probably a week away from going to that big Dairy Queen in the sky when he walked into the kitchen after his nap. There was his wife, putting a stick of butter in the corn.

"What are you, trying to KILL ME?" he asked.

Her awkward and painfully long pause answered his question. Then he made a lifesaving suggestion. "Maybe we should go out to eat."

That was two years ago. Despite the fact that she tried to kill him the Betty Crocker way, they are still married, still golfing, and, believe it or not, her life is much better. He still drives her crazy, but now he can't trust her in the kitchen, so as a compromise they eat out every meal. Most often at their beloved country club, where they appear to be the perfect couple.

She tried to take him out and wound up with a lifetime of takeout.

She's on Easy Street; he's on Atkins.

THE DOCTOR IS IN, THE PARKING LOT

Affairs

The PTA president was asking for someone to approve the minutes to the previous meeting when a mother I knew stood up and pointed her index finger as if it were a Glock at another mom halfway across the cafeteria. "Stay away from my husband, you slut!" she snarled.

Simultaneously another woman stood and said, "Approved." Was she approving the slut comment or the minutes? I just know the next item of business, the book-fair budget, was dull in comparison.

A friend of mine was once married to a rather wealthy New Yorker, who entered their marriage as a model husband, until he started dating a runway model, then a flight attendant, then a bank clerk.

When his wife found out and confronted him, **he** was the angry one. "If you were a better wife, I wouldn't need a girlfriend!" he declared.

That marriage was doomed; the minute the wife realized that his latest girlfriend, their nanny, was on their payroll, she instituted a new rule: none of his girlfriends would get a salary and a paid vacation from her. They split.

Another couple was just returning to the grocery-store parking lot, after he'd forgotten French bread, when the wife announced suddenly in an urgent voice, "We have to go!"

"Why?" he asked.

"Let's just go, now."

"Why?" he asked again. "We just got here."

"Because my father"—she pointed at the car straight ahead—"is making out with his doctor."

Inside the bucking Buick were her father and the female psychiatrist he'd found in the Yellow Pages to help him through a problem in his marriage. I wonder if she was charging him for the hour in the parking lot.

I know a family that decided to install a beautiful fifty-thousand-gallon in-ground swimming pool. They had the hole dug in March, and to make sure that she was in poolside condition, the wife joined a nearby health club to get into shape. "If the neighbors are gonna see me," she said, "I'm going to look good!"

She obediently went to the gym every day, and the pounds melted away. She got hooked on weight training, she had more energy, she looked forward to things for a change, and she looked terrific. Her husband was delighted.

The day they were to open the pool for the season, the husband came home and found a note on the kitchen table explaining that his now shapely wife had fallen in love with a guy at the gym and was moving to Texas with him. She hoped he'd understand, and left an address to have her mail forwarded.

P.S.: You can keep the kids.

He did, and wound up becoming a better father because he also had to be the mother. Six months later in Texas the buff bride married her gym-rat boyfriend. They had three positively blissful months, until he left his new wife for the Pilates instructor at their new gym.

Once a cheater, always a cheater.

Danger Signs Your Spouse Is Having an Affair

- Throws away frayed underwear, upgrades to animal prints
- Starts working out, asks, "Do you know where I put my abs?"

- Calls to say, "I'm working late tonight," even though he's been out of work since Vanilla Ice was in the Top 40.
- Has lipstick stains in nonlipstick-stain area
- Phone bill reveals six hundred text messages last month from 976-HOTGIRLS (don't jump to conclusions; he could just be addicted to porn)
- Husband turns up in a supermarket tabloid with another woman (see next page)

MRS. HAPPY'S ADVICE

Affairs are so sad. One day you think you're happily married, next thing you know there's a boiled rabbit in your kitchen stockpot.

Because every marriage has 750,000 moving parts, chances are yours will eventually hit a pothole. Sometimes it knocks your front end out of alignment and you need to get professional help. That's why ministers and priests and marriage counselors and bartenders are standing by to help you through the rough times.

Remember the unknown philosopher who said, "Love is grand, but divorce is a hundred grand."

WHEN IT HITS THE FAN

Kathie Lee and Frank Gifford

Their storybook marriage hit an iceberg. An allegation was made that Kathie Lee was running a sweatshop in Honduras with kids at sewing machines belting out her line of clothes. "I never had a factory!" Kathie Lee protested. "If you don't have a factory, you can't hire any workers, so how could I have had a sweatshop?"

Three months after the initial accusation, the man who'd charged her as a sweatshop operator wrote her a letter of apology, but it was too late, the damage had been done. "Not one news organization printed the apology."

She and her husband, Frank Gifford, an NFL Hall of Famer and longtime **Monday Night Football** play-by-play guy, battled the sweatshop allegations for a year. It "personally hurt" them to be accused of being child abusers just as they were about to open a seven-million-dollar home for AIDS and crack babies, paid for with their own money. They were sick and tired of being kicked around by the world press.

"Let's take all this sweatshop money I supposedly have," Kathie Lee joked, "and buy an island someplace." She may have entertained the idea of running, but she couldn't hide from what came next. A supermarket tabloid ran a picture of Frank and another woman at a ritzy New York hotel. Was it an affair? "No," Kathie Lee insisted. "It was a one-time stupidity, not an affair. He didn't know that woman. She was hired to do it."

She may have been hired, but her husband did go into that hotel with her. "It was the deepest betrayal possible," Kathie Lee told me.

She and Frank had fought the sweatshop allegations together; now Frank **was** the problem. And she was faced with the question of what to do about a husband who cheated on her. Should she stay with him, or call a really expensive New York divorce attorney?

She wrote about her choice in her song called "Bitter or Better."

I can be bitter or I can be better
Strange how it depends on just one letter
The "I" is the difference, the choice can
be mine
What am I going to choose this time?

"The hurt was devastating. It will probably be a scar on my heart all of my life." And so she struggled along. She knew plenty about divorce; she'd gone through one years earlier after a little-known marriage. "We never should have gotten married," she remembered as she thought back to the day of her first wedding, to a man who'd been her Bible-study group leader. They shared the same values and beliefs and thought they were perfect together. And yet, Kathie Lee said, it was doomed from the start. "I realized my wedding night...That should say it all."

Back then many women were expected to be a combination June Cleaver and Betty Crocker. "I was a good girl, from a good family, and divorce was not an option. You made a vow, you stuck it out."

"I slept in the guest room for five years," until he moved out while she was on tour with Bill Cosby. Burned badly after that first divorce, Kathie Lee knew a second divorce would be devastating to her family—she had two small children with Frank. Finally advice from a professional helped her make up her mind whether to stay or go: "If you can't forgive your husband, forgive your children's father."

She stayed with Frank.

"Had it been typical behavior for him, I would have divorced him. But because it was so aberrant and so out of character for him, I weighed the joy he brought to me compared to the heartbreak. And there was no contest when it came to that."

So what is her advice to all of us when life smacks us between the eyes? The key to a good marriage, she told me, is the key to a good life: "Put God first" and life will follow.

Amen.

One More Thing: Double Trouble

Kathie Lee Gifford has a perspective on men that is unique. She's been through so much. Married and divorced, then remarried with two children, and twice she's been in the eye of a category-5 tabloid hurricane. Let's add one more thing to her résumé: bigamist.

Remember, for many years she was married to **two** men at the same time. At home her husband was Frank. Meanwhile, Regis Philbin was her TV husband. During her Vegas-style show she'd say, "I think I'm the luckiest woman in the world. I get to work with Regis Philbin and go home to Frank Gifford.

"Thank God," she said with a giggle, "it isn't the other way around!"

MOTHER OF ALL ARGUMENTS

The Prenup

When I got married I signed two official documents: a marriage license and a Missouri state fishing license. Our Justice of the Peace was also a game warden and he was having a two for one sale. I was broke at the time, looking forward to the honeymoon, and the last thing on my mind was the chance that one day I'd have to split my vast wealth with my future ex-wife. At the time I was more concerned with my new fishing license. "Does this cover carp?"

"Would you ever get married without a prenup?" I asked Donald Trump. "No," he instantly responded.

The number one reason married people argue is money. So it's probably a smart idea to settle monetary issues up front, because nothing turns Mr. Thrifty into Mr. Crabby faster than an unexpected $974 credit-card bill from Dress Barn.

Prenups can be about anything. Usually it's money or kids, but in the world of celebrity, many very famous household names have their lawyers spell out in no uncertain terms what they'll expect to happen in their marriage. I've heard of prenups in which a famous woman allowed her husband to watch only one football game per Sunday. Some stars insist on mandatory sexual positions. And another image-conscious celebrity limited his wife's weight to no more than 120 pounds; anything over that and she'd forfeit $100,000 in property. "Step on the scale.... Oh, one forty?... There goes your S-Class. Honey, step away from your Mercedes...."

For at least three generations the Trump men have asked their women to politely pen a prenuptial. "My father asked my mother to sign a prenup! Do you know how many years ago that was?" A lot. Raoul Felder was still knee high to a bailiff, when the Donald's father Frederick C.

Trump asked Mary MacLeod to marry him in the middle part of the twentieth century. Back then prenups were about as common as black matte U-2 iPods. And yet his mother knew exactly what his father was asking her to do. "She wouldn't sign it!" the Donald says. But the Donald's father eventually caved and married her anyway. Good thinking. They were married sixty-three years sans prenup.

"She wouldn't do it for the right reason by the way," Donald continued. "There are two types of women, a woman who will sign a prenup, and a woman who won't sign. The women who won't are broken into two categories. People who are looking to rip you off, or people who feel from a love standpoint, it's the wrong thing to do." His mother was the latter.

Here's an important point, Donald adds, prenups aren't good just for guys. Many women earn more than their husbands, and they need to cover their assets. You don't have to be loaded to benefit from a prenup, although you may have to get your spouse loaded to sign it.

- WARNING: Asking somebody to sign a prenup is dangerous. They will think you don't trust them, or that you're only concerned with money, not love. Because asking to sign is sure to generate unusual anxiety, **never** ask your intended to sign when they have the

following items in their hands: a javelin, a pitchfork, a battle ax, a Jedi light saber, or an improvised explosive device.
- P.S. Don't be surprised if a casual "prenup talk" results in not getting lucky any time soon.

How would Mr. Trump suggest you bring up this touchy subject? "Darling, I love you very much, but just in case it doesn't work out, here's what you're going to get." The Donald has an "it's just business" look on his face as he says, "It's an ugly agreement, a horrible thing to bring up to a woman." He's right. I'd rather tell my wife that "In this light you look like Jim Belushi" than prenup her.

"Nobody gets married thinking they're going to get divorced, but fifty-eight percent of the people who get married get divorced," says the Donald. "In this modern-day society, with a very problematic court system, with the sleaziest lawyers in history, with terrible people, if you don't have a prenup, you're doing yourself a great disservice. I have friends who would be very poor, anguished people today, if they didn't have a prenup."

While Donald Trump's father couldn't get his mother to sign one, Donald trumped the three beautiful women he married by insisting they sign on the line before he walked down the aisle. When the first two marriages unraveled, he was lonely, but he had the law on his side.

"I had a very rough time with Ivana. She went after me unbelievably. But I won. The prenup totally held up. With Marla, same thing. I won. If I didn't have it, I'd have liens on Trump Tower, liens on all my properties. I couldn't do any of the things you have to do in business!"

And if he didn't have those prenups? "I wouldn't be here talking to you today, unless you're talking about whatever happened to Donald Trump."

Yes, without prenups Donald Trump wouldn't be the Donald Trump we know. He might be the night manager at a Midtown Manhattan KFC, barking at the chicken: "You're fried!"

MRS. HAPPY'S ADVICE

Before they got married, Paul McCartney's wife, Heather Mills, asked if he wanted her to sign a prenup. He apparently didn't feel the need. Four years later they split with a giant sucking sound of millions going into Heather's very large purse.

Most first-time brides and grooms don't ask the other to sign a prenup because, just like Sir Paul, they believe their love will overcome all obstacles. Besides, most first-time marrieds don't have much community property. Who really wants Uncle Ned's Barcalounger? "I insist, you take it, remember I threw up in it."

My advice? Talk about it before marriage, so that once you're wed, you won't be angry that you didn't bring it up. Remember, prenups are to marriage what the cup is to a baseball player. You've got to protect the family jewels from a curve ball.

chapter seven

Happily Ever After

CRACKING THE CODE

The Secret to a Long, Happy Marriage

I know this brilliant guy who's been blessed with a great sense of humor, has an amazing analytical mind, and is a legendary litigator. His clients are some of America's largest corporations as well as some of the country's highest-profile citizens. Forget his formal title, he's a fixer. His job is to make problems disappear. He is a confidant to one of America's great political parties, and on top of all that, he's been happily married for more than thirty years.

"What's the secret to a happy marriage?" I asked him.

"Are you kidding?" he asked. "That's easy." And then he launched into a PowerPoint-like presentation about how important it is that both husband and wife have similar senses of humor, respect for each other, an interest in each other's work, and plenty of tolerance.

"But of course there is one single-most important thing…" He paused.

I was on the edge of my chair; this would be the Holy Grail from the smartest guy I knew.

"The secret to a happy marriage is…separate bathrooms."

The meter was running and so he continued. "Separate bathrooms let people conduct their private business in private. Separate bathrooms let people keep their stuff in its own place, their own way," reducing the chance of things going missing. Where the hell is my Jean Nate?

And finally, separate bathrooms keep the "territorial imperative intact." Think of it as an invisible line in the tile.

This was not theoretical. Apparently one of the ways he and his wife had gotten through decades of marriage smoothly was that not once did he ever find her panty hose soaking in his sink.

As soon as America's couples realize that having separate bathrooms is one of the keys to a good marriage, home remodeling will skyrocket, with millions taking vacant walk-in closets or idle space and turning them into private bathroom sanctuaries. As soon as I stop typing, I'm calling Morgan Stanley and sinking all of our savings into porcelain futures.

"YES, DEAR, POUR ME A BEER"

The Longest Marriage on Earth

This is a question that has puzzled all of the great thinkers of our time—Dr. Laura, Dr. Phil, and Dr. Dre: How long does love last?

According to the Guinness World Record keepers, Percy and Florence Arrowsmith were married for more than eighty years.

What kept the Cal Ripkens of couples together?

"I like sherry at lunchtime and whisky at night," Florence confessed.

No wonder Percy digs her—she's lit half the day.

But there's more to love than a borderline blood-alcohol level. Florence said, "You must never go to sleep bad friends."

From my perspective that's sound advice. Many a wife has gone to bed so angry with her man that she intends to smother him in his sleep, only to fall asleep herself and then wake up the next morning completely clueless as to why she wanted to exterminate her mate the night before.

Florence has a caveat to her "Don't hit the sack cranky" credo—that neither husband nor wife should ever be afraid to say "Sorry."

Elton John sings, "Sorry seems to be the hardest word." What does he know? He's not married to a woman.

Meanwhile, Florence's husband, Percy, doesn't need liquor or lyrics—to him the secret to marital bliss is two words: "Yes, dear." Wiser words were never said. How many times would feelings not have been hurt, or egos bruised, or nostrils sent a-flaring, if only one of the feuding parties had simply been a bigger person and totally defused the situation with a "Yes, dear"?

MR. HAPPY'S ADVICE

If you rewind that wedding tape that's sitting in your hall closet, you'll see that nowhere in the wedding vows do you pledge that whenever there's a disagreement, husband and wife must battle to the death to settle it. Sometimes you've just got to cave and say "Yes, dear," and sometimes you've got to say "Sorry." This is especially hard for guys who as children were referred to as Mr. Smarty Pants and have now grown up into Mr. Know-It-All.

The choice is yours: you can fight to always be right, or you can go with the flow and compromise to find a happy middle place. I have been in situations

where I was **right, and yet for the sake of my marriage, I would agree that my wife was. She has done the same with me.**

Don't think of it as "Sometimes in life you have to shut up and simply eat a load of crap." Think of it as a choice. Rock the boat and try to prove you're right, or go for the smooth cruise and wind up a happier person.

That's why I say to my wife (who is statistically more often correct than me), "I'm sorry" or "Yes, dear." Because I love her and I'm in for the long haul. Besides, if this works out, she'll be with me when I'm 105, which will be great because I'll surely need somebody to tell me where I left my teeth, and whether my rug is on backward.

HONEYMOONER HALL OF FAME

Real-Life Success Stories

I asked my wife why she thought we'd made it this far without one of us cutting the other's brake cables. At first she said, "I dunno." Two days later she had thought about it and had an answer.

"The thing that makes our marriage work is that my husband makes me feel like I'm the most beautiful girl in the world, every day." I found that particularly touching because I'm that husband! And I meant it.

She could be in a police lineup with those Victoria's Secret angels and, if given the chance to choose one, I'd pick my wife. I'm not interested in kissing any Victoria's Secret models, especially now during the cold and bird-flu season. A kiss can last fifteen seconds, but strep throat lasts a week.

A retired Alaska Airlines pilot told his future daughter-in-law that the secret to his long marriage was simple: "I was only there half of the time." He'd been married for twenty-seven years, and half the time he was in the sky, or waiting to fly somewhere. It was bad that he was gone so much, but it was good insomuch as he wasn't around enough to drive his wife nuts. "Honey, return your tray table to its full upright and locked position, NOW!"

Donald Trump said there are two key kinds of personal happiness, business and family. "I know people who are very successful in business, but they've got nobody to go home to. I know people who have people to go home to, but in business they're failures, and they're not happy.

"But I also know people who have a lot going on...but they're not healthy. I think happiness starts with health. If you don't have your health, you're not going to be happy."

A very famous television journalist who's from a family of very long marriages said that in her family, a successful marriage is easy, if you've got the right components. "Respect. You've got to **like** each other, in addition to loving each other. You've gotta be genuine, and have a sense of humor. My mother (married almost forty years) and my grandmother (married sixty-two years) see their husbands as very funny men, who still make them laugh."

She went on to say that one of the early mistakes many make is getting involved with somebody who they don't completely like. There may be a part of their personality that drives them crazy, but they'll think, "I can fix that."

"Don't get married young!" a network broadcast executive told me. "I think there should be a law that nobody under the age of thirty can get married." She makes the case that once upon a time people got married after high school, but that was when life expectancy was sixty. Now, thanks to lotions and potions and better lifestyle habits—"Step away from that cheeseburger, Chubby"—people easily live into their eighties and beyond. "What are the odds that you can tolerate someone for fifty years?" she asked. "The chance that two people are going to change in complementary ways is almost zero, so it's best to wait until you are 'done' before choosing your mate."

She summarized with brutal honesty: "I realized my husband was a good mate for me when it dawned on me that I would never have dated him in my twenties."

"A successful marriage is all about rounding out the edges," a friend told me. We all have peccadilloes and personal weirdness that make us very unattractive at times. When you "round off the edges," what you're really doing is leaving 90 percent of a person as is. But the 10 percent that bothers you can be rounded off by either telling your partner "Please stop that!" or simply looking past it.

One of my wife's oldest friends has been rounding off the edges for years. "We argue all the time," she said. But those annoyances are quickly dealt with. "As my boys say, I'm going to do what I'm going to do anyway, so get over it." With a prosecutor-like summation she made her relationship recipe easy to understand. "We know that sometimes we are going to anger the other person. But we're not wasting money on therapy. I'll tell him 'You're nuts' and he'll leave. It works for us. We've never been happier."

PEGGY SUE GOT MARRIED

Marrying Your High School Sweetheart

Why is it that in high school the strongest, most handsome and talented guy always goes out with the school's most beautiful smart girl?

"That never works out in the long term," my philosophizing high school sophomore declared. Oh really, my young Aristotle on the iPod?

Richard Bruce was born in Nebraska's capital city, Lincoln. His father was a soil-conservation agent for the U.S. Department of Agriculture. When Richard was twelve his father was transferred to the faraway land of Wyoming.

"That first summer when he lived in Casper, he didn't have any friends," recalled his first girlfriend, Lynne Vincent. "He was playing baseball, but he was also reading his way through the history section of the Carnegie Library. And I was going down there and I was reading my way through the fiction section."

Despite long late hours lingering at the library, they didn't cross paths at the reference desk; they met as juniors, the old-fashioned way, in the locker-lined halls of their school. Their senior year Richard was the senior class president and captain of the football team; Lynne was the homecoming queen and baton twirler. You've been in high school, you know the math, of course these two were dating.

Lynne remembered their first date. "We went to what was known as a formal dance in those days." It was held in the Izaak Walton League's log cabin. The attraction between the two was apparently immediate. How did she know he liked her better than the homecoming queen first runner-up?

Duh. "When he asked me out on the second date."

They started spending a lot of time together, including almost every Tuesday at a place called the Canteen, a building that had been built for World War II and was later officially restored as the local teen hangout. It was over Ping-Pong and dancing to skipping forty-fives that they realized that there was something special between them.

"I sometimes watch that movie **Peggy Sue Got Married**," the former Miss Vincent told me. "It was a little like our lives."

In the movie, Peggy Sue was the it girl in high school, very popular and always in demand. She fell in love with her boyfriend, Charlie, and they got married. But later in life Charlie ran off with another woman. That's where the parallels with the young Wyoming couple end.

In real life after they graduated from high school Richard did run off, to Yale on a scholarship, and Lynne went to Colorado College. Yale is a long way from the big blue sky and rolling mountains of Wyoming, and after three semesters at Yale, he dropped out. He was homesick and he missed his baton-twirling girlfriend.

"There was never any big hiatus in the relationship," Lynne told me. "It was a pretty steady relationship, and we got married in 1964."

Back together, they both worked very hard and accumulated impressive résumés. She got a master of arts and a Ph.D. President Ronald Reagan appointed her chair of the National Endowment for the Humanities. She hosted a network television show and became a very successful writer, speaker, and author.

Her husband returned to university life and received a master's in political science. He was almost finished with his requirements for a doctorate but left for a one-year fellowship in the office of a congressman from Wisconsin. He would eventually work in the Nixon and Ford White Houses before putting his political knowledge to good use, being elected to serve the people of his home state for a decade. He went back to the Executive Branch when President George Herbert Walker Bush tapped him to serve in his cabinet, and he later ran a Fortune 500 company. In 2000 a longtime family friend, George W. Bush, asked Richard to join him in a run for the White House. In a squeaker Bush got the top job and Richard Bruce Cheney was vice president of the United States of America.

"I love those stories," Lynne Cheney told me about their long lives together. "They're full of nostalgia. But the most important part might be all the time we spent with books in the Natrona County Library."

Like many couples, they had something in common from the get-go—a deep love of the printed word. Lynne Vincent Cheney spent one summer long ago reading her way through the fiction section, while her future husband quietly perused volumes over in history. Now they're both part of American history.

They have two grown daughters, and grand-children, along with a forty-plus-year marriage. Mrs. Cheney knew the topic of my book and offered this: "If you're trying to come up with formulas for good marriages, I do think that having a great backlog of shared experiences is a real bond; it's hard to create in other ways."

A backlog of shared experiences.

She's right. How often do you hear "We have a lot in common" as an indicator of a couple's compatibility? Being from the same place, having similar interests or occupations. Both being hooked on guacamole and salsa chimichangas. Whatever.

Having a lot in common initially gets your foot in the door, but it's over the arc of time that those interests translate into shared experiences. They're the things we remember, the times of our lives. "The fact that we have so many experiences in common, so many stories to share, so many friends that go back such a long way. Such affection for this town in Wyoming where we grew up. For the people and the teachers who we knew there."

Let's recap: Shared experiences + course of time = real bond.

We are all from our own Caspers somewhere on the map; the road to now has been littered with amazing victories and tragic flameouts. If you're the only one (aside from your relatives) who knows your personal story, what good is that? We are a needy species. We need to share. We need someone beside us for the journey. We need the validation of somebody important in our lives loving us unconditionally, and, when appropriate, being brutally honest. "Lay off the cabbage, it's almost bedtime."

THE 4-H CLUB

Recipe for a Happy Marriage

When I was a kid in Kansas I belonged to an organization that taught me how to raise pigs and rope steers: the 4-H Club. The four H's stand for heart, head, hands, and health.

Now that I'm older and married, I've got four new H's: honesty, handling, humor, and handcuffs.

None involve barnyard animals. Yet.

Honesty

Liars always get caught, and cheaters never prosper. So why bother? Besides, if I need to tell you why you need to be honest, you're unreliable and not to be trusted, and somewhere on your hard drive you've downloaded "101 Excellent Excuses for Knocking up the Swedish Nanny."

Handling

We don't mind doing the fun stuff, but when it comes time to get serious, we get scared. You can't just put your head in the sand and pretend you're not jealous or angry or retaining water; you've got to handle problems as quickly as possible. If it bothers the woman that her husband still washes his mother's hair, that's something that must be handled promptly—I would suggest before the conditioner is applied.

Humor

Some people never laugh. Like the pope. He's got a serious job, and the last thing a billion Catholics need is to see the pontiff with a Steve Martin arrow through his head. But you're not the pope. So from time to time, you need to cut up a little.

Last year my wife had a total knee replacement. As she was checking in to the hospital for the surgery, the admitting clerk asked if she knew she had a significant risk of death by stroke or heart attack. She did not. Then he asked if she had a living will. Nope. "Who will make the decision to take you off life support if you're incapacitated?" he asked. She pointed to me and burst into tears. When he told me the private-room charge was not covered by insurance and it was an extra twelve hundred dollars a day, I burst into tears.

In the waiting room, she worried aloud, "Who will raise my children?" "Which of the neighbors will try to move in on my husband?" and "Did I leave the curling iron plugged in?" We were in a stage-five pity party. Time to change the mood.

I took her hand, looked her right in the eye, and said, "I know you're worried. It's a big operation, but it's not a heart transplant!"

I had just touched my toe on matrimony's third rail. She squinted at me for a second. I knew she was about to either go straight into an uncontrollable river of tears or...

She smiled, then giggled, and then in a huge release of emotion let out a loud laugh. The others in the waiting room were looking at us as if to say, "What's so funny?" Hey, loosen up, trick-knee patients. You're not having a **heart transplant**!

Ninety-five percent of all couples say that humor is an important aspect of their mate. However, humor is tricky. It can go either way. That well-intentioned joke could just as easily have been interpreted as a thoughtless line, and my wife could have grabbed a scalpel and gutted me like a trout.

My wife is a joker as well. When I turned thirty, I developed a wild hair that just shoots right out of my right earlobe. Between haircuts, it can zoom out an inch or so. My wife doesn't refer to me as Sasquatch or "the missing link." She's more subtle. She'll get real close to that ear and whisper, "Hold still, I'm gonna floss!"

Handcuffs

Think of the handcuffs as the ties that bind. Once you handcuff yourself to somebody else, you'd better be ready to throw away the key forever. More important, be happy with whom you're cuffed.

Review

Honesty + handling + humor + handcuffs = Mr. and Mrs. Happy. Maintaining this equation is not easy. It's tricky and sometimes elusive. But if your heart is in it, and your spouse's is too, and you work at it, odds are you'll be successful. However, if you're not willing to put in the time and energy, you may wind up with a broken heart, which could eventually lead to a heart transplant, which of course trumps knee replacement.

WHERE'S THE TABASCO?

How to Keep Marriage Exciting

We all get bored. Even the really exciting stuff gets old after a while. My sources tell me that even XXX-rated adult features eventually become a little ho-hum by the time the "actress" in the French-maid outfit runs out of gas in the driveway of the fraternity house.

Some may think that a French-maid costume would spice things up. My wife says it "would be all right, as long as it's worn by an actual French maid, who could clean up under the sink."

But we really shouldn't need outfits and stunts to keep our marriages exciting. I believe that the best investment you can make in your marriage is face time. I know we're all busy, but if you don't find time to be together, why did you get married in the first place?

Married life is like a casserole. A bunch of ingredients are stirred up and prepared with care. In the beginning it's served hot. But after a while, the dish cools to room temp, and you've had it three nights in a row. You don't want to get to the "Leftovers, again?" stage.

The key is to treat your spouse like he or she is special to you. And if you're looking for a great idea, may I suggest a simple act of kindness. Totally surprise your spouse by doing something unexpected, something that says, "Hey, Hot Stuff, you're special!" Personally, the most expensive thing that I can give my wife is my time. So here's what I do.

Once a month I come home early and take my wife to lunch. It's great. We spend time together, have some laughs, talk about things we don't want the kids to hear about, plus I get a hot meal and sometimes even dessert!

And there are two additional benefits. We often see her friends at another table. They wave and say hi, but when they spot us lunching and giggling, they get jealous. "Why doesn't **my** husband come home and have lunch with me? Who's he having lunch with? I bet it's that tart from the Help Desk!"

If you're busy, there are other ways to show you still have a pulse. Write a letter or poem (avoid haiku at all costs). Whatever, it doesn't really matter. It sounds corny, but it really is the thought that counts, even if it's a subscription to the Bacon-of-the-Month Club. It shows you care about your spouse's feelings, if not her/his cholesterol level.

We are basically lazy. Keeping your foot on the gas all the time was tedious, so Detroit came up with the cruise control. Pilots needed to flirt with the flight attendants, so they invented the autopilot. And because we're too lazy to ask for directions, MapQuest. "I told you it was a **left**!"

It's easy to **get** married; it's hard to **be** married. It's easy to get up, kiss your spouse, go to work, and not spend one second of the day thinking about your spouse again, until you walk into the house: "I'm hungry! Make me a sandwich!"

We've all got to try harder. That means putting down the newspaper, turning off the Internet, muting the TV, turning to each other in a quiet room and just starting to **talk**.

Don't just talk about the routine stuff you talk about all the time. Try to dig something out that you didn't know. Remember when you first met, how **everything** was new and intriguing, how you once found everything about each other sooooo charming? Now you've been together a long time, you probably feel you know all your spouse's answers, so you've stopped asking questions. Trust me, you don't.

THE NOT-SO-NEWLYWED GAME

Five Questions for Your Spouse

1. Have you ever phoned in a bomb threat?

2. What movie star would you ditch me for?
3. If the house were burning, what one thing would you run in to save?
4. Have you Googled an old flame or looked up his number in the phone book?
5. What one habit of mine would you change if you could?

NIAGARA FALLS PLUS FIFTY

Good News: Love Lasts

The idea for this book came from a family trip to Maui two summers ago, when we realized that we'd just flown five thousand miles to a place that was crawling with newlyweds. We saw hundreds of them, still picking the rice out of their hair, fawning over each other, carrying on at the pool as only newlyweds would. To my wife and me, having been there, done that, albeit long ago, it seemed so familiar.

"These people have no idea what they're in for," my wife said with a giggle.

"No clue," I concurred as I ordered a piña colada to celebrate the fact that I'd just figured a way to turn this Hawaiian vacation into a tax deduction.

Our next vacation was to Palm Beach, Florida. We went because it's a quick flight from New York and because my resourceful wife found some really cheap airline tickets. Okay, there were some restrictions. At first the kids were required to fly below in a sky kennel, but we upgraded them later to the ski rack on top of the plane.

I quickly discovered Palm Beach was perhaps the best vacation destination possible for a person writing a book about being married. One night around six, we wandered back into our hotel lobby and discovered it was ground zero for early bird dancing. We sent the kids to the room to order a nine-dollar Disney movie that we already owned, and we plopped down in the last empty chairs.

"That band is terrific," I said, scanning the crowd and realizing that we were the youngest by at least twenty-five years. Then, over the course of an hour, I figured out that this was the place where the people who honeymoon in Maui today will wind up retiring in fifty years. Because fifty years ago these people were honeymooning at Niagara Falls, but tonight they were here with us, wearing their sensible dancing shoes.

No disco, no electric slide, no rap—the music made us feel like we were in a time machine and perfectly matched the dancing demographic. Mitch Miller, Bing Crosby, and when it was time to go crazy, Perry Como. The songs they'd fallen in love to, performed live again for them to hear, provided they had their Beltones cranked up.

The instant the band started, every couple jumped to their feet to dance. Despite arthritis, hip replacements, and the fact that it was way past their bedtimes, this was a night of romance.

"It's Viagra dating," one waitress told me. Whatever it was, it was terrific to see that forty, fifty, sixty years after they walked down the aisle, they still had the heat.

"They're playing the McGuire Sisters!" said a man who'd spent the previous three minutes carefully reading the label to the nonalcoholic tea, to make sure it was also decaffeinated. "Let's go, Tookie!"

Then, to the waitress, he said, "Give me your phone number. If this keeps me up, I'm calling you at three A.M.!"

There was a seventyish gentleman who could barely stand, and yet he was dancing with his bride—from a walker. The most amazing thing about this couple of seasoned citizens: their smiles. Great big, genuine smiles. As they closed their eyes, they mouthed the words to the songs that were taking them back in time from here and now to then and there, to a time when they were young and healthy and just in love. Nobody here could run the mile in less than ten minutes, including me; they were not in the same shape as when they first got married, and yet gauging by the smiles and how close they were dancing on the slow numbers, and the tender looks they gave each other, they were clearly still in love.

It reminded me of a story Kathie Lee Gifford once recounted to me, one she'd heard from a friend about a conversation he'd had with Billy Graham. He'd asked the reverend how his wife, Ruth, who had been having serious health problems, was doing.

"She can't sit, she can't stand," Billy Graham told the friend, listing a litany of health problems. Then with a twinkle in his eye, he said, "So we continue our romance with our eyes."

There comes a time when our internal love machines are still working but our bodies wear out.

At the conclusion of the evening, which we thoroughly enjoyed, I made a pact with my wife that we'd return in twenty-five years, for the high-fiber appetizers and a jaunt back in time. Where else would we be able listen to a Muzak version of "Dancing Queen" by Abba?

It was inspiring to see what it looks like when marriage works. This was their victory lap. They'd been through ups and downs, triumphs and defeat, and yet through all the years, they stayed together. To them "Till death do us part" meant something.

After the band returned from their break, they started another set. Five, ten seconds into their song, every couple was heading back to the dance floor.

I'd heard "Our Love Is Here to Stay" scads of times before, but it wasn't until that night, seeing these couples, that I finally saw what Nat King Cole had been singing about all along. "Not for a year but ever and a day."

I'm Almost Out of Toner

FINAL THOUGHTS

The end of a book is a daunting piece of real estate. I asked my wife how this book should close, and she said, "Would it make for a good story if I died?" I started laughing because that's how Hollywood would end this love story.

MOVIE TREATMENT: The author's wife meets an untimely death as he composes the final chapter of the book at his gleaming Apple iMac. She'd been reading over his shoulder when a chunk of blue ice fell from a 747 passing overhead. The debris crashed through their roof, hitting her squarely on the top of her head. A year after the funeral, the author accepts the Nobel Prize for literature in Stockholm; he's surrounded by his grieving children on the dais. When presented his award, he raises the trophy as the **pop pop pop** flashes from the motor-drive cameras carve out an eerie silhouette on the stage curtain. He pauses and looks upward as he dedicates this honor to his fallen missus.

Author: "Honey, thanks for the great ending."
(Thunderous applause, as the crowd quietly digs into their pockets for Swedish Kleenex.)

FADE TO BLACK

Attention, Hollywood, my wife's not dead, thank goodness. And she'd better not check out any time soon, because winter's coming and somebody has to shovel the driveway.

Here's what I need to say here at the end. Thanks.

Initially I wanted to write this book because I wanted to retell some of the amusing stories of married life. But a funny thing happened on the way to the punch line: I realized a couple of things about myself as a husband.

We are taught in America, the world's only superpower, that BIG is important. But having spent a year collecting and recollecting the stories in this book, I've realized that the most important things in my life were **not** the big things. I've won Emmys, I've gotten jobs hosting network television shows, and I once saw Tom Brokaw naked (don't ask)—all big things to some.

But now, with the wisdom of age and experience, I find the important things, the things that mean the most to me, are the little parts of life that happen every day. A first kiss, a newborn baby, or the hilarious place your dog pooped in the yard of your jerk neighbor. Nobody in the world would think any of that stuff is important, except you and your beloved. And now I know, that's the way it should be.

Real life is a mosaic made up of ten gazillion little bits. Each day another piece gets glued on the wall. It's so subtle, so tiny, you don't really see the fullness of the life you've lived until you stop for an archaeological family flashback.

Personally, we've had trouble at our house. My mom died on Christmas morning; that's a tough one to get over. My wife's had a five-year struggle to pain-free mobility thanks to her knee problems. She has been a trouper and a very good sport. I joke with her about the things married people kid around about, but it's just that, a joke. To me, she is just perfect in every way. That's why it hurts me that she's not 100 percent recovered. Walking up our stairs is no big deal to me, but every step she takes is a painful reminder that she's part titanium.

When I was about halfway finished writing this book, my son graduated from high school. For his party (with rental tent and moon bounce) I made a film of his life. Like most parents, I'd been videotaping all of our family's big events for the past twenty years. After taping, I'd promptly take the cartridge out of the camera, put it on a stack, and forget about it.

There is a certain magic to watching a rerun of your life. On tape you may be twenty-five, but you're watching it twenty years later. You've forgotten a lot. What you wore. Where you lived. The gait of a little boy. The squeaky voices of your kids on their first day of school. It took a full month to watch all eighty-four hours of videotape. The verdict: we have had, on balance, a very happy life. Seeing it, I wound up with a sense of satisfaction that I'd accomplished something good. And my wife agrees: we've had a good life together.

Many people are so busy that they never take time to pause and look at the arc of their lives. It's human nature to fixate on the bad turns we've made. My fear is that if somebody **never** looks back, they'll never see the good stuff. If they do, they may agree with me: they've had a happy life. Then again, they may see something that they hadn't noticed before. Something fixable that they can make better in the future. It's like a chapter review where you say to yourself, "This isn't working, but it's not too late." Or "What was I smoking? We've got to sell this chinchilla ranch!"

In a couple of paragraphs when you're finished reading, I want you to think about **your** life. The funny times you've had together, the tough times when you leaned on each other. Rewind that tape in your head or get out the family movies and sit down and watch. It's not exactly a do-over, where you can redo something in life that's gone awry, but it is your chance to see where you've been, while knowing all the while exactly where you'll wind up.

Up close, daily life is a blur, but there's an unusual clarity when you look in the rearview mirror.

I hope you see a life that's had its share of happy times. I hope in tough times you were reliable and dependable and so was your spouse. I hope you can appreciate your loved one's good traits and happily tolerate the parts that bother you to high heaven. Speaking of heaven, I hope you see the fingerprints of a power higher than any of us.

I hope you see all that and more. If so, my work is done.

One final personal note. Yesterday I was supposed to tell my wife that I was out of wearable socks and ask if she'd buy me some more. But I forgot to ask her. At three-fifteen this morning, I opened my sock drawer, expecting to grab a mismatched threadbare pair, but instead I found a dozen pairs of brand-new socks. I hadn't asked; she just knew. Remember what I said a moment ago, it's not the big things in life that mean so much, it's the little things.

I'll thank her when she calls me here in the office shortly. That's when I'll tell her that I accidentally took my car keys **and** her car keys to work, and she's got no way to pick up the children after school. She's going to kill me.

So maybe somebody does die at the end of this book after all.

Author Thank-yous
and Shout-outs

Behind every Mr. Happy is a Mrs. Happy, so I must start by thanking my wife, Kathy. After work, when I was busy writing and talking to myself, somehow the kids got dressed in clean clothes, driven to and from school, the bills got paid, the meals were made, and life went on, all thanks to her. I love you, honey, now make me a sandwich (our private and frequent joke... although I am hungry).

The original Mr. and Mrs. Happy are my parents, Jim and JoAnne Doocy. I owe them plenty for teaching me what a rock-solid marriage looks like. Also to my four beautiful sisters, Cathy, Lisa, Ann, and Jenny, and their families. I'm glad I can provide support (nonfinancial) whenever needed.

Peter, Mary, and Sally (PMS), you are the best children a father could ever want. You've made us proud, and I know you will always be there for your mother and me when we need that big monthly payment for our luxury assisted-living-for-seniors home.

To the visionary Fox News chairman Roger Ailes, the greatest boss in the history of television news, thanks for giving me the job of a lifetime. Also, to Beth Ailes, who hired me years before Roger invented Fox News. Thanks for bringing me and my family to New York and launching me into the five-cups-of-coffee world of morning television. Roger and Beth, you have both changed my life forever. I can never say thanks enough.

Also to Fox senior big shots Jack Abernethy, Bill Shine, and Brian Lewis, thanks for the support, especially after the unfortunate "Xeroxing incident" at the Christmas party in 2004. Thanks as well to Irena Briganti in the publicity wing for all the helpful guidance. And a special thanks to top Fox lawyer Dianne Brandi who read this book before it went to the printer and later said, "Hannity had better punctuation."

I'd like to thank a few familiar names to breakfast-time television viewers: Brian Kilmeade, E. D. Hill, and Lauren Green. Also Andrew Napolitano, Kiran Chetry, Alisyn Camerota, Dr. Georgia Witkin, and Tiki Barber. Thank you all for your daily support at my real job.

Cheers to those at Fox not usually seen on camera (other than grocery-store surveillance): Ron Messer, Marvin Himmelfarb, Christine Thoma,

David Clark, Maria Donovan, Paulina Krycinski, and Gary Schreier. Thank you for your input. I'll never tell the supply guy you're all stealing copier paper.

Thanks to super lawyer Bob Barnett for the legal stuff. I loved hearing all of the juicy off-the-record stories about the private lives of all your famous clients. Just kidding. Don't worry, Bob Woodward!

To the anonymous celebrities who told me their stories of marital mayhem, thank you for trusting me. If you want to make sure I don't put your names in the paperback version, please negotiate with my agent for the movie rights.

To the few celebrities mentioned by name in this book: Donald Trump, Erica and Geraldo Rivera, Kathie Lee Gifford, and Mrs. Lynne Cheney. I was honored that you shared your stories. Special thanks to the assistants who helped with logistics: Christine Gardner, April Isenhower, and Rhona Graff-Riccio. And to the assorted celebrities who didn't care if I used their names: John Wayne, Sean Astin, and Richard Simmons, who broke my nose but not my spirit.

To my personal friends who've spilled their happily married secrets: Mary and Jack, Todd and Madeline, Kathy R., Anne, Mark, Tony and Christie, Tony and Phyllis, Kent, Mike and Judy, Goldie, Peter and Blanche, Jim and Mary, Rodger and Beverly, Faith and Ray, Matt and Rachel, Martha, Peter (Noriko), Gary, and finally Bob. Thanks for your friendship and love.

To the publishing professionals at William Morrow who turned my original manuscript (handwritten notes on cocktail napkins and match covers) into this beautiful book. Thanks to Mauro DiPreta, Joelle Yudin, Lynn Grady, Pamela Spengler-Jaffee, Richard Aquan, and Michael Morrison.

Also thanks to my in-laws, Rob and Gwen Gerrity, Dub and Randa Gerrity, and Big Daddy Joe Gerrity.

Thanks to Father Giles Hayes, Paul and Muffin, Ann and Andy, Greg, Washington Palm, West Coast Jen Lingua, Worldgate Tennis Club, McCormick & Company (maker of paprika), my recreation league baseball team of 2001, and Charlie.

To the best man at my wedding, Alan Schroeder, thanks for standing on my shoe so I couldn't run. I guess you knew it'd all turn out just fine.

And finally thanks to all of you for buying and reading this book. It has been a dream my whole life to write a book that somebody would read to the end. You just made that dream come true.

About the Author

STEVE DOOCY is an Emmy Award–winning broadcaster and the co-host of **Fox & Friends** on the Fox News Channel. He has earned reporting and writing awards from the Associated Press, Sigma Delta Chi, and the National Academy of Television Arts and Sciences, and has worked at NBC, CBS, and Fox. He and his wife, Kathy, live just outside New York City with their three children and high-maintenance dog. (And they really are happily married.)

"Visit www.AuthorTracker.com for exclusive information on your favorite HarperCollins author."